THE INDISPENSABLE GAME OF X'S AND O'S:

How I Learned Everything I'd Ever Need to Know
about Life by Playing High School Football

KEVIN McLEMORE

Certificate of Registration Number: TXu 2-157-828 Registration Decision Date: September 23, 2019

ISBN: 978-1-6847-1840-5 (sc)
ISBN: 978-1-6847-1841-2 (hc)
ISBN: 978-1-6847-1844-3 (e)

Library of Congress Control Number: 2020902364

Lulu Publishing Services rev. date: 04/06/2020

This Book "The Indispensable Game of X's and O's" outlines perseverance and decision making that exactly parallels success as an entrepreneur.

This book will be a great encouragement to anyone engaged in the struggle to create excellence in business.

Jeff Allen President, Northwest Translations, Inc

The Indispensable Game of X's and O's:
Everything I'd Ever Needed to Know About Life, I learned by Playing High School Football

Reading this book feels like I am having a conversation with Kevin. His inspiring and encouraging passion for people to be their best shines through in every chapter. The anecdotal and practical advice helps to unlock your true potential and purpose. Makes me believe, if he can do it so can I.

It gives you the permission and power to transform the way you live. This book takes you on a life changing journey. "This is a must-read for young people and adults."

Robin Banks-Sneed RN, MSN Clinical Nurse Educator

The Indispensable Game of X's and O's invited me to look into the window of Kevin's life and see what happened when his pain and circumstance encountered truth. His captivating journey is beyond encouraging and reveals the truth about us all- we are all created with divine purpose to impact others for good and to overcome every struggle, yet it is our choice to pursue this truth or allow the lies of "circumstance" to be the boss. The truth is, we are all born to win, and it is trumpeted throughout Kevin's journey.

Kristen Broughton, Founder & CEO
Purity & Grace, Pure Chocolate Energy
www.PurityandGrace.com

Kevin's profound insight seeps through every chapter. His words transcend all cultures, all ages, and all walks of life - giving every reader the opportunity to see the surrounding world from an entirely new lens. Truly an epic read that is nothing short of soul capturing.

- Alexandra Barone
CPT, Municipal Police Academy Graduate Of 16', Current MBA
Graduate Student, and Prospective Law Student

This is the story of a young black man, abandoned by his mother, ignored by his father. Despite the best efforts of his grandparents and uncle, he is skating by in life, neglecting school and drawn to the call of the street. When he unexpectedly finds himself on the practice field for high school football, he throws himself into the beauty of the game and the team, and adopts the values the sport, at its best, instills: self-knowledge, courage, honesty, integrity, singleness of purpose, practice, practice, practice…

McLemore relates his circumstances, his choices and the principles which guided him to become a good father, trainer and inspiration to those around him. Among many moving incidents is the description of McLemore observing his infant son, curled in the fetal position, holding his dreams to his heart. A moving, inspiring read for young readers and for those who think they have nothing more to learn.

Cynthia Verges, J.D., M.A.I.P.S.

If you find yourself saying "I'll never succeed at this", then read this book!

We've all faced our own battles and the author's courage ignites a flame that inspires us to drop the excuses and start pursuing our dreams.

His story is powerfully moving, vividly drawn, and keeps its energy to the very end.

I enthusiastically recommend this book for anyone interested in overcoming adversity with faith, belief, and getting a helping hand along the way.

YAY!!! Best of luck, Kevin!!!

Best regards,
PJ Cline, Marketing Consultant, Public Speaking Coach

McLemore's book is a deeply personal narrative of a boy's difficult choices during his formative years, and how those choices played into his development as an athlete, father and mentor. A slight freshman, McLemore stumbled into the bruising world of high school football and learned lessons of dedication, persistence, and sacrifice that inspire him to this day. His values, woven into life anecdotes make compelling reading, and will inspire readers to improve both physically and spiritually.

The words may be gone after you've finished your journey with him, but the ideas will remain.

Brian Haber, B.A., D.D.S., OMFS

Throughout my life, I have had the pleasure to get to know and learn from Mr. McLemore. At first, he started as my mom's trainer, then became my trainer, then became a mentor and teacher in valuable ways for me. He taught me from his life experiences, such as never giving up and pursuing your dreams. These have proved to be valuable for me so far in my first year at Wake Forest, and I can truly say that he helped prepare me for this experience through his words and actions.

The Indispensable Game of X's and O's allowed me to see more in to Mr. McLemore's life and learn about where he came from. Reading about his difficult upbringing and his resilience to overcome adversity gave me even more respect for a man whom I already greatly respected. Mr. McLemore's story of his life and learning the "System" is extremely motivational and enlightening. Thank you, Mr. McLemore, for being open and allowing me to learn more about your life. "Tyler Perry needs to read this book".

-Luke Grycewicz, Wake Forest Class of 2023

If you're looking to gain wisdom, discipline, self-reliance and resilience? Look no further, this book is it. Whatever stage you're at in life whether it be young, middle aged or old, if you want to improve yourself, let this book's principles be the building blocks you use towards becoming a better version of your previous self. Kevin's gritty tale and lucid writing only increases your tenacity and hunger for improvement. Soak up every page, every lesson and use it to guide you through the inevitable twists and turns of life. A pleasure and privilege to read but more importantly a message to us all that we can always improve our life if you're willing to put in the work.

Maukan Mir
Graduate student in Industrial Psychology

While many of the stories in X's & O's are set in the world of athletics, the lessons learned are universal. You don't need to be an athlete for them to register with you. Some of the topics are more serious, but there are many laugh out loud moments. You will find yourself cheering on a little girl who doesn't have limits, because she doesn't think that she has any. The book is a good read that will give you plenty of food for thought.

Susan Vekony
Booking & Funding Analyst
Wayne, PA

FOREWORD BY MELISSA L. SHUSTERMAN

I have known Kevin for over nine years. I often ran into him at the local gym and was amazed by how he always, regardless of the weather or personal exhaustion, exudes a welcoming positivity when addressing acquaintances, colleagues and children. Kevin has a knack of making everyone feel heard and feel special. Little did I know that this clear outlook came from a personal decision, in his teen years, that would change his life forever and create the man he is today. At age 14, Kevin was active with a crew of young troubled adults that were masters of getting into kid trouble. He took his natural skill, speed, that helped him run from the neighborhoods "Hoods", and turned it into a remarkable ability to run a football field with stealth speed and nimbleness.

How I Learned Everything I'd Ever Need to Know About Life by Playing High School Football by Kevin McLemore is one of those books that urges you to pass it along to your neighbor, friend or co-worker after devouring. The book is about the lessons Kevin learned while playing high school football for the 'Mighty Teddys.'

McLemore is thrown into the world of endless training, drills and competition. What Kevin takes from this challenge, is the opportunity to be molded and influenced by mentors while at the same time creating a personal philosophy of personal responsibility that he carries with him to this day.

"There are two kinds of people: Those who truly want success, and those who are simply trying to avoid failure. I vowed to always strive for success. I was determined to be a Mighty Teddy." - Kevin McLemore

Kevin is a generous storyteller and the reader experiences every hit on the football field, every turn of events in his life firsthand. He shows us how others influenced him personally and led him to achieve his personal success. He gives credit to his Coach for challenging him and helping him hone his philosophy of life. Coach is full of encouraging words that a young Kevin soaks up to help him win games and that later help him deal with the challenges life throws at him.

This is a book that everyone trying to reach a goal can relate to. So, if your running your first 5k, running for office or trying to start a business, the lessons in How I Learned Everything I'd

Ever Need to Know About Life by Playing High School Football by Kevin McLemore will guide you, inspire you and keep you on track.

Enjoy.

Melissa Shusterman
Mother, wife, sister, daughter and small business owner
State Representative, 157th district, Pennsylvania

ACKNOWLEDGEMENTS

I am sure the view I have outside my window today would not be what it is if not for the many teachers, coaches and self-fulfilled mentors who impacted my life and kept pointing me in a direction that made my life extraordinary. I would like to thank all of you, not in any particular order:

Freshman and Varsity Coaches, Joe Russo, Tom Clemens, Tom Montgomery, Head Coach Mike Haley. My Mighty Teddy teammates at Roosevelt High School classes of 74-75 and my teammates and coaches that made the road trip after the announcement of the closing of Roosevelt High School in 1975 to Dayton Roth High School, who I graduated with in 1977. I cannot begin to say how much I appreciate all the life lessons I learned early on and the priceless memories we all share which helped mold me to be more today than I was yesterday. Please note, I would like to list everyone who had an impact on my life back then, but it would be another book. I hope you know who you are because I am thanking you with more than just words.

I would also like to say thanks to some amazing men and women that are in my life today who I just love. You are the people that sometimes put your life on hold to suffer through the many drafts of not just this book, but the other books I've written that are waiting to be released. No one ever played their fight song louder than you all do. Thanks Lisa Robertson, Nancy Grycewicz, Brian Haber, Cynthia Verges, Meghan English Thorburn, Vicki Rush, Jodi O'Neil, Michael Block, PJ Cline, Jeff Allen, Darlene Daggett, Les Brown "My mentor" Patty and Ed Kersner.

Thank you to my Lifetime Fitness family, who endured and witness, day in and day out, the many life lessons I attempted to pass along to anyone within ear shot of my voice. "Leah Gibian" Use your gift and sing "Dream Big" your voice is your "Y."

Without family, this story would be a bunch of words on a page with little to no real meaning. So, I would like to thank my brothers and sisters who help mold, entertain and support me as a child and the man I am today. Love to my late brothers and sister, Dwight, Anthony and little sister Ronda, may God be with you. My sisters Daria, Yolanda, Tonya, Tammy, Theresa, brothers Dwayne, Leroy Jr. and Raymond. I love and am so proud of all of you!

DEDICATION

It would be irresponsible of me to say the life I live today was created all on my own. Writing a book about myself and sharing my life's experiences may sound bragi and sometimes I wondered if anyone would really care.

Well, Leroy McLemore Sr, "my father," Norma Jean Lartigue "my mother", William (uncle Bill) Daniels, Joseph and Annie Phillips "my grandparents" Betty and Roney Green "cousins" and my baby brother Raymond Neil McLemore, all care.

All the above people were extremely influential in adding to the pieces of who I am today. Without their encouragement to live a dynamic and purposeful life I would have become just another sad story that would never be told. So, those life lessons started with all of them preparing the world for me.

I am nothing without my family and outside of God, my family always comes first. My children, Lakisha, Alexander, Theodore, Jillian and Connor (Who is like a son) are all amazing people the world should get to know. They have heard me say countless times that I have to get the world ready for them and nobody will ever love them more than dad. I love them all unconditionally and I hope what I have written within the pages help them understand their dad better today than they did yesterday. Maybe some of my words will become parts of their conversations with their children.

So, although the list of people I thanked or dedicated this book too is long, it without saying I am at a loss for word when it comes to how grateful I am for Monika Hill, who at times is tougher on me that many of the people I'd played against. I am sure I will one day write another book, telling her story. If for whatever reasons this does not happen, I hope these words show my gratitude for believing in this dream.

SPECIAL THANKS

Daralyse Lyons, "my editor" effortlessly held my hand, stood on my chest and looked at every scenario of my life, my words, my actions, to get the best version of the story I was trying to tell in this book. You challenged me, and I know you would say it was the opposite. I am truly grateful for your gift and friendship.

The best security in life in your ability to produce consistently, which you do, with no problem. You rock!

CHAPTER 1

HOW IT ALL GOT STARTED

When I began to keep a daily journal, Elvis was on his comeback tour and Richard Nixon was our nation's 37th President. I, on the other hand, was nothing but a young punk standing at one of the many crossroads in my life with my middle finger high in the air, intent on proving to all who doubted me that I didn't care what any of them thought. I wasn't going to continue to be controlled by my environment. I was going to take control of it.

When I was growing up, I thought I was the only one who had my set of problems. In fact, my story wasn't that different from the guy's next door. My parents divorced when I was in the third grade. My mother packed her bags and headed west to Beverly Hills 90210. My father got custody of my brothers, my sisters and me. Not long after the ink on the separation agreement dried, my dad moved us into his parents' home. It was my grandparents who acted as my parental role models. They taught me the fundamentals of a day's work for a day's pay, which I now call trading hours for dollars. And they offered love in the form of philosophical musings, practical advice, and supporting our basic needs, while my dad was busy drinking.

Like so many young African American men, I was raised in what society once called a "broken home" and now refers to as a "dysfunctional environment." To me, it didn't matter how anyone described what was happening in my house. What mattered to me was finding an answer to the question "What did I do to make my parents stop loving each other?"

I didn't understand that my mother and father were ill-equipped for love. I thought I wasn't lovable enough. I didn't have the right clothes, live in the right neighborhood, or go to the right school. Daily, I encountered those who, instead of referring to me as Kevin, Kev, or even K, called me "Boy" or used an even more pejorative word, which I will not repeat but which starts with an N and with which I am all too familiar. My eighth-grade teacher told me I would never be anything more than a janitor.

In single-parent African American households, the fathers are typically the ones who leave, and, although my dad wasn't exactly father of the year, he was a constant in our lives, which I later came to see as a rarity. At the time, however, none of the seven of us kids ever felt lucky to be statistical anomalies. We didn't want a mother who abandoned us and a father who stayed around. We envied people who had moms and dads in the house. We also envied those who never had to worry about whether there'd be food on the table.

Although we never knew it until the U.S. Census Man came around, my family was poor. Even after the report was released, we denied reality. Never mind that our father had defaulted on the mortgage and lost our little piece of the American dream at 559 Cedarhurst, or that the seven of us McLemores had to move into his parents', our grandparents', house (where we stayed until the day I went off to college), we didn't see ourselves as welfare-worthy. We didn't see ourselves as the N-word either. What we did see was a world in which everything that was good was classified "white" and everything that was wrong with the world was painted by prejudice and described as "black."

Those who were supposed to uplift us through encouragement and education judged us instead. As I look back at the moment my teacher prophesized what she saw as my inevitable future, I smell her stale coffee breath and my fists ball up involuntarily. To say I was angry would be putting it mildly. Her words put an exclamation point on my resolve never to live down to others' expectations.

Pops used to say "Life rewards action, your action will either make your life, or action will cost you your life"

Pops had a brilliant mind and a lot of wisdom to impart. Unfortunately, I had ADD/ADHD – although they didn't call it that then. There was Special ED, but in order to qualify for separated classes, or extra academic help, you had to have an obvious limitation. As far as anybody knew, I was inattentive. Whenever Pops launched into one of his little speeches, I'd get bored and wander off or find myself daydreaming too much to internalize all of what he was saying. If I had, I'd never have taken a pocketknife to two of my teacher's car tires. In my mind, she deserved it. I'd show her I could be more than just a janitor. I could be a vandal…

Letting my anger lead me stopped me from realizing what I'd later come to see as obvious – proving her wrong would have been much more satisfying than getting even in an underhanded way. I didn't just get even. I got caught with the knife in hand.

As my reward for my tire-slashing retribution, the principal expelled me and the cops gave me a free ride home. On the way from the school to my grandparents' door, the officers chided me for my bad behavior, but Dayton's finests' lectures were nothing compared to my grandparents'. When the officers left and Pops and I were alone, my grandfather ordered me to strip down to my shorts then took off his belt and let me have it, after which he banished me to my room.

"That's nothing!" he shouted as I dragged my sore butt upstairs to the attic bedroom I shared with my brothers. "Wait until your father gets home!"

I wasn't about to wait for my dad. I excused myself to go to the bathroom where I crawled out of the tiny window where, to my surprise, I collided with my unsuspecting father. Dad had been walking up the steps of the house at the precise moment when I scrambled out the window.

"Where do you think you're going?" he asked.

Caught in the act of escape, I had no choice but to follow him inside.

I often wonder what would have happened if I'd stayed around longer, or daydreamed less, all those times my grandfather freely shared his wisdom. If I had paid more attention, would I have still chosen to poke my teacher's tires with a pocketknife? I like to think I'd have come up with a better plan.

Pops always said life either punished you for doing what you shouldn't be doing, or rewarded you, and held you up as an example, for doing what was right. Yet another of his lessons I didn't internalize until after I started playing high school football.

Long before I got into the eighth grade, I started doing the wrong things. I was angry with my parents for splitting up and, although I couldn't have articulated it at the time, I was acting out as a result of feeling abandoned and unloved.

Everyone loved my dad, Leroy. He was one of the best-looking men that ever walked this earth. He had it all – a great body, a smile that could light up Bourbon Street, and light brown eyes that would've humbled the great Billy Dee himself. It was no surprise that my mother would be so enamored with him that she'd give birth to four of his babies. She'd already had three of her own, all of which he accepted as his own. It was a good thing, too because, when she packed up and left town without notice, leaving all of us behind, Dad raised the seven of us the same. Not that that's saying much. He was more attentive to the bottle than his kids.

In my mind, I never felt wanted by either of my parents. My mother escaped to California and even though my father lived with us, he wasn't, it felt like he was more absent than present. Still, instead of walking away when life got tough, he put us in a safe, clean, loving environment – his parents' house.

As much as I loved my grandparents, I longed for a two-parent, problem-free existence. I was naïve enough to believe there was such a thing. Now, I know that, if I sat in a room with 100 people, everybody in the room would have some version of a tragic story.

I was a child who felt abandoned by his parents, but that didn't mean my pain was worse than anybody else's. I don't have to look any farther back than my ancestors for examples of those who had it worse.

My ancestral history began on the lower deck of a boat that my ancestors had to row themselves. Even though they were heading away from home toward a place that promised only punishment and pain, they rowed. If they refused, they'd have been beaten to death and their bodies would've been tossed in the sea as shark bait. They arrived in a new and unfamiliar world only to be separated from their loved ones, beaten, chained and sold on auction blocks along with the pigs (and the pigs boasted higher prices). Even after they were set "free," because of Jim Crow segregation laws, there were still policies that restricted what they could and couldn't do.

Some might argue that I was born behind the eight ball, yet I've come to believe that when our mother left us and our father skirted his responsibilities by escaping into the bottle and pawning us off on his parents, my parents were introducing the seven of us kids to what I now define as "The System." "The System" is the not so secret secret to life. We can either make it work for us or against us.

My father seemed content with his role within the system, but I didn't want to go on record as being another black child living in what folks called a broken home. I lived out my entire childhood telling anyone and everyone that the reason my brothers and sisters and I were living with our grandparents was because our mother had died. Back then, no one was presumptuous enough to ask for details, so I was able to successfully lie to those around me without worrying about getting tripped up on the particulars.

The more times I told someone she had died, the more dead she became in my mind. Even though I said, and a part of me actually believed, that my mother was "dead to me," my heart ached. Somewhere deep within my gut, I thought I wasn't lovable enough for her to stay.

I was lucky though. I had people that were always there for me, with plenty of life's wisdom, insights, and love. My grandmother was the rock for the whole entire McLemore clan. She was the nucleus. I called her Mom and everyone else called her Mamma Annie. My grandfather, Joe Phillips and my late Uncle Bill were my first lifeguards. They provided a foundation I have come to appreciate, although I once took it, and them, for granted. They told me I was no trust fund baby and that the only way to get by in life would be to study "The System," then to work with it, rather than against it.

I was a sucker, they said, if I thought I could do something tomorrow. Tomorrow wasn't here yet, and yesterday was a history lesson that, once learned, would be easily forgotten. It was what I did with my time right now that defined who I was and what impact I would have on the people around me.

I listened to their stories of how far they had to walk to school in their day, with holes in their shoes, no hats, coats, and nothing but a nickel in their pocket for a peanut butter sandwich and milk, which they would trade for a sandwich made from hobo meat (bologna). But I didn't always pay attention. More often than I care to admit, Pops' and Uncle Bill's words bounced off the walls in my head. They had purpose. They were determined that nothing was going to stand in the way of what was rightfully theirs in life. And they were intent on imparting all their hard-won knowledge to me. Unfortunately, I was too shut down to absorb all the brilliance they were attempting to convey. Fortunately, despite my inattentiveness, some of their messages filtered through.

Uncle Bill was like a father/big brother/best friend all rolled into one. Pops was like a big rock in the middle of a super highway, secure in his place, daring anyone to move him, not caring if his presence was an inconvenience. I was a little afraid of him. I wasn't afraid of Uncle Bill. He could read me like a brand-new Marvel Comic book. He knew my pain without my ever uttering a word. It wasn't just me either. He claimed anyone could read what was in another man's heart by reading his eyes.

One day, being the "smart ass" that I was, I asked him to look into my eyes and tell me what was in my heart.

(Warning: If you have an Uncle Bill or anyone like him in your life, don't ever ask this question if you're not prepared to hear the truth).

Uncle Bill's pale green eyes bore into my dark chocolate ones. His breath tickled my nose. I inhaled the scent of toothpaste and shaving cream.

"Before you ever begin to think of yourself as something great," he told me, "you must kill that demon that makes you second guess yourself. If you want others to respect you as a person, you must respect yourself first. Develop what's inside." He poked his finger into my chest. "This is where your character lives. What's inside there is an important part of 'The System' of life. Make peace with what's in there and everything else will begin to fall into place."

At the time, I lacked the capacity to understand what he was telling me. I was convinced I had all the answers and that no one knew what I was going though. Now, at sixty, with the filters of youth, invincibility, false pride and self-righteous rage stripped away, I know that no truer words were ever spoken. Sometimes, when I'm feeling nostalgic, I'll raise a hand to my heart, place it where he touched me and understand that he knew the me I used to be better than I knew myself.

Pops was more insightful about life's principles and people than anyone I've ever met. He may have only been armed with an eighth-grade education (because he had to help raise and provide for his brother and sisters, he dropped out of school), but he read more books than people with doctoral degrees. He believed young folks should take advantage of every opportunity for a good education, both in the classroom and the world.

At 5'7", he walked with a deliberate purpose, head held high, and a self-confident look that said, *I may not have a formal education, but I'm a well-read student of life.*

The thing that I remember most about Pops is that he always had a book in his hands. Whenever a topic arose, whatever it was, he'd read a book about the subject and could therefore contribute to the conversation. It seemed as if his ability to read extended beyond the page. He'd be talking to me and looking up at the sky, as if he could decipher words written in the clouds.

Despite his ready access to information, he wanted to equip all seven of us grandkids with the skills to think for ourselves. So, in addition to his little lectures, he'd inspire us to arrive at our own answers. Once, he sat me down and asked me a series of questions:

Can people trust you to always do your best?

Are you sincerely committed to the task at hand?

Do you sincerely care about other people? If so, do your actions support that?

Do you have purpose? A reason to do something that will make life better for someone other than yourself?

Without waiting for my reply, he walked out of the living room, into the kitchen, sat down, and began drinking his coffee, leaving me to ponder over the seeds he'd sewn.

No matter how much Pops and Uncle Bill tried to enable me to question my motivations and evolve beyond my limitations, the streets called to me as loudly as the siren that warned everyone there was a storm coming.

I couldn't explain it, but it was a feeling in my gut that compelled me to use my sister's eyebrow pencil to draw a thin dark line above my lip and sideburns down the side of my face. I started hanging with the kind of fellas who never got an invitation to any parties but showed up anyway. I wasn't sure why they were so defiant, but I was filled with what I thought was justifiable rage and I felt at home surrounded by other angry outcasts.

It wasn't until the night these so-called friends and I were shot at by a gang that called themselves the Chains of Rap Brown (Dayton's version of the Crips and Bloods) that I realized that the road I was on was leading in one of two directions: a dead-end life with no meaning or purpose, or death. I should've known before that night, but I told myself I was entitled to do what I wanted. I ignored the nagging voice inside that sounded a lot like Pops when, during a conversation with my elder brother, Mac "Leroy Jr" and me, he said, "If you stand on the right side of the law, you'll never have to worry about the law standing against you." It struck me as a nice thought, but even as a young black man, I'd already figured out that the law seemed to be more comfortable with its boot on my chest and its finger on the trigger than with me standing by its side.

Like any other black male youth, I learned early that there was white law and black law. Black law… I thought about Martin Luther King and all the atrocities we were seeing on the news. But my grandfather had blind faith in "The System." He wouldn't listen to anything anyone said against it.

"Don't try to defy 'The System,' Kevin," he told me. "No reason to make life harder for yourself than it has to be."

Hard. I wanted to be hard. Yet, as I tried to outrun a .38 being shot into the darkness, I could feel whatever toughness I thought I had running down the inside of my pants. It didn't even dawn on me to be self-conscious about peeing my pants. Not when I was running for my life.

My friend, Jason "Bully" Kirkland, was the first to leap over the fence of Westwood swimming pool. As usual, I was right on his heels.

Jason was the toughest guy in our neighborhood. He could whip anybody young or old. He was the "friend" that taught me how to steal liquor from my grandparents' house, that stood beside me, each of us taking turns being lookout while the other picked the lock on someone else's bike. He was also the "friend" that suggested we beat down the kid who'd beat down a member of our crew. I trusted Jason as much as I could trust anyone. He was my best friend and, when we got to high school, he would turn out to be one of the toughest kids on our football team. Any time we were on the verge of a serious situation, Jason was the one I looked to.

He ducked low and we slithered on our bellies into the adjacent women's bathroom, where we hid and hoped…

I can still smell the acrid odor of gun smoke and see pieces of metal and dust falling around us. With every pop that hit the wall, I could hear the bullets calling my name. "It's only a matter of time before I find you, Kevin McLemore," each one said. "When I do, you'll think twice about beating up another member of the Chains of Rap Brown."

It didn't matter that my friends and I had only been retaliating. (One of the Chains of Rap Brown gang had beaten and robbed one of our friends). This was a high-stakes game in which we'd inadvertently engaged. They'd shown their hand. We'd tried to call but, instead of seeing our bet, they were upping the ante.

Pops used to tell me that a good run was better than a bad stand. That night, I figured out what he meant.

"Stay down low," Jason hissed.

How much lower could I get? I was face down on the ground of the girls' bathroom floor.

I used to complain whenever my grandmother came out on the porch and yelled for us to come in, to beat our eight o'clock curfew. Now, I prayed, "Grandma, please call me home. I want to come home."

I no longer cared what my friends thought. Not even Jason. I wanted to live more than I wanted his approval. I mustered up enough of whatever I hadn't dropped in my shorts, picked myself up off the bathroom floor, and jumped back over the Westwood fence. This time, Jason followed me. For once, instead of running toward trouble, I fled from it.

Jason wasn't far behind me, and not far behind him were the Chains of Rap Brown. Shots rang out. *Bang! Bang! Bang!* As I zigzagged my way across the Westwood football field, I could have sworn I felt a bullet whiz past my ear.

Even though I had taken a path that led me to a game of chance with the Chains of Rap Brown, that night, I learned two things: I wanted to live more than I wanted to die, and I was fast.

I made it home safely. Jason did, too.

Neither of us told our parents, or, in my case, grandparents, what had very nearly happened. We didn't talk about it at all, except to each other.

My dad used to say that, if he asked each of his children to run to the edge of a cliff to determine our fate, my brothers and sisters would run close to the edge, then stop and look over to see how far they stood to fall, whereas I would run as fast as I could and leap into the air, never once pausing to see what I was leaping into. I would jump blindly. He said I always knew I was going to land on my feet. I wasn't so sure. Often, I did land on my feet, but, even when I didn't, I knew I'd be okay. Life had been knocking me on butt since birth. I only had two choices: stay down or get up.

CHAPTER 2

BE TRUE TO YOURSELF

Walter Payton, one of the all-time great running backs in pro-football, passed away on November 1st, 1999. I admired him as a connoisseur of truth and vulnerability. After his only Super Bowl appearance – which his team won – Payton sat on the sidelines and cried. He didn't cry because he was overwhelmed by his team's accomplishment, but because he had failed to score a touchdown in the biggest game of his life. When a reporter attempted to console him by saying he would have another shot at it next year, Payton replied, "Like I always told you guys, tomorrow is promised to no one." He acknowledged that sometimes reality could break your heart.

Although I told a lot of truths, I also told my share of lies, sometimes out of willful rebellion and sometimes because there were things that hurt so much, I couldn't be honest about them with myself.

My grandparents used to tell us that the truth would set us free. Whenever they suspected us of mischief, they'd assure us that, if we fessed up and were honest, our punishment wouldn't be as bad as if we lied. We bought this hook, line and sinker. And my little butt (which, by the way, wasn't so little, then or now), would be too sore to sit on for all that truth setting me free my grandmother rained down on me. With time and age, however, my butt got tougher.

Summer was coming to an end. My mother was still living somewhere in California. I was still maintaining she was dead. Bright-eyed, bushy-haired (I sported an afro), pants hanging low on my butt, Chuck Taylors white as white could get, I was ready for high school.

Roosevelt was the biggest public high school in the city of Dayton, Ohio. It was the same school my father and his brother attended. All my brothers and sisters before me went there. It sat in the middle of the block on Third Street, directly across the street from Blue's Barber Shop, JoMo's (where Ripple and Mad Dog 20-20 were the preferred cocktail of the local residents), and a little donut shop where we'd order hot, glazed donuts, full of all that nice, rich, fatty stuff that everyone is trying to stay away from nowadays. Home to the Mighty Teddies, the school had two swimming pools, an indoor track, a couple of gyms, and a reputation for having one of the most celebrated sports programs in the city's history. After Lucinda Adams, an Olympic gold medalist sprinter, won the 1960 Olympics, she came to Roosevelt to teach. We idolized her.

High school was my first real step into adulthood. From an early age, I'd heard over and over again that anyone who wasn't gainfully employed at age eighteen, or away at a full-time college, had to either pay rent at home, plus a portion of the gas and electric bills, or move out and get a place of his own. My grandparents' policy was set in stone. There would be no negotiation. I had four years in which to get ready to make it as a man.

As I sat in physical education class, I wondered how many of my classmates were wondering what they'd do if, after graduation, there were no jobs and no higher education scholarships, or student loans.

Just a few months earlier, I'd been a naïve kid who thought he knew more than he did. But after that night at the Westwood pool, and now that I was in ninth grade, I realized that, if I was going to make it out of high school and into the real world, I had to stop screwing up whatever possibilities came my way and start taking responsibility for my life and my choices.

It probably sounds as if I was my parents' and grandparents' worst nightmare. Au contraire. I was the apple of their eyes. I did what was asked of me at home, worked a job so I could have my own spending money, respected my elders, and tried to dress as nicely as I could, given how little money we had. I played the role of Perfect Son, and Grandson. Outwardly, anyway. But the Kevin I exhibited to others didn't synch with the Kevin in my head. I was like two people operating at cross-purposes, sharing one mind.

There's an old television show, "The Twilight Zone." One day, I was watching it when a disembodied voice came on the airwaves and said, "There is no twilight zone of honesty. A thing is right or wrong, it's black or it's white. The gray areas are reserved for those who bend the truth."

For a very long time, I operated in the gray area. It helped me cope. It didn't help me be someone who could look Pops or Uncle Bill in their eyes without worrying they might see what I was afraid to acknowledge. My mother had voluntarily abandoned us.

The gym doors opened. Coach Renee Russo walked onto the hardwood floor. A respectful quiet fell upon the room. He motioned for my class to take a seat on the bleachers. Dressed in his red polyester coach's shorts and white polo shirt, slightly balding and speaking with a very thick Italian accent, Coach Russo studied the room. It was a co-ed class. He began to take roll.

James Jackson, Jason Kirkland, Pamela Jones, James Smith, Fran Lewis...

When he called out their names, each responded with a steady "Here" and a raised hand.

My name echoed through the gym. "Kevin McLemore!"

"Here."

I expected Coach Russo to continue to the next student, committing them to memory, yet he called off the rest of the names on the attendance sheet without his baby blues ever leaving my fear-filled face. Why was he examining me so intently?

When rollcall was finished, Coach Russo gave a short speech about what he expected from his PE students. I tended to tune out during even the most riveting of adult-delivered speeches, but his tone demanded undivided attention. After he finished laying out the particulars of what was and wasn't acceptable gym class behavior, he asked for a show of hands of how many of the young men in our class planned on going out for the freshman football team.

My eyes scanned the raised hands. I had no intention of playing football. I'd never so much as seen a game. But I noticed that, whenever a hand shot up, Pam Jones, one of the prettiest girls in the class, and several of the others would ooh and aah. It didn't matter that we were indoors, and there was not breeze to be found, Pam's wavy brown hair seemed to be blowing in the wind, back and forward, and then back again.

A force overtook over my body. I couldn't stop it. It pulled my right hand toward the heavens. Coach Russo made another note on his clipboard.

I had no plans of following through on my hand's promise, but the smile on Pam's face was worth my little white lie. Her expression said, *if you make the squad, I'll be at every game, just to see you play.* That's what I wanted it to say, anyway. Turns out that, for all four years of high school, Pam Jones never even noticed me.

There are two statements from the movie *Forrest Gump* that remind me of the me I used to be. In the first, Tom Hanks, playing a character called Forrest Gump, says, "Life is like a box of chocolates, you never know what you're gonna get." Lying to myself was fast becoming a box of chocolates. No one knew what I was going to say next. Heck, I didn't know. The other statement, made repeatedly throughout the movie by Gump's character, but attributed to his Mama, was "Stupid is, as stupid does."

What I proceeded to do was, without a doubt, one of the stupidest things I'd ever done, yet it would prove to be the best worst decision of my life. When I got home that day, still having no intention of trying out for Roosevelt High's football team, I continued my earlier lie.

"I'm going out for the football team!"

I made the big announcement to my brothers and my dad thinking I'd impress them. On the contrary. Dad took a magazine from the coffee table and disappeared into the bathroom. All my brothers, except Little Mac, wordlessly dispersed too.

Little Mac studied my 134-pound meat-and-bones frame and smirked. "So, you're going to be one of those guys who run up and down sidelines holding the yard marker to one of those goal posts?"

In retrospect, it was probably my family's lack of enthusiasm that compelled me to keep up the ruse. I didn't want them to see me the way I saw myself. I told everyone who would listen that I was going to make the team.

My grandparents filled out the try-out permission slip, which I never turned in. I came in from school every day, changed clothes, and ran off to who knows where for a couple of hours, returning just before dark and acting as if I was pretty sure I'd make the squad. For a person that supposedly went to try-outs every evening for almost week, I managed to keep my clothes spotless. Never once did I come home complaining about being sore, nor did I ever break a sweat. I would have if I knew what was in store. But, how could I?

Never in my wildest dreams did I think my notoriously disinterested dad would take off from work to come watch me practice. Not only did he call out of his second shift job to see me, he brought a friend with him. Mr. Williams, the father of Big John Williams, one of the varsity squad's legendary "greats" was my dad's best friend and a huge fan of football and Dad seemed to want to show me off. It would've made for a great Kodak father and son moment if not for one tiny catch. Dad didn't have a son on the team he could watch practice.

I didn't have the heart to tell him I'd lied to impress a girl, then kept the lie going in the hopes that it might make him and the rest of my family proud.

In the back of my mind, I heard my grandmother's voice. "The truth shall set you free, but your daddy's gonna kill ya."

Before getting into his car, I tried nearly everything to stall my dad. I even said he didn't have to give me a ride because I planned to run there as a warm-up. He wasn't having it. Holding the rear door open, he yelled at me to get my little black butt in the car. I did what he had asked.

How did I get myself into this mess? I thought. *Maybe it's best if I come clean.*

As I rode in the backseat of my father's car, mentally chiding myself for raising my hand in gym class, and praying for an act of God to come down and save me before my dad and Mr. Williams dropped me off at football practice, I had no idea how I was going to get myself out of the situation my lie had gotten me into.

A lot of things ran through my head on the way down to the practice field, including contemplating jumping out of a moving vehicle. It was a good thing Dad didn't ask me for directions. I had no idea where the field was, having never been there. Mr. Williams knew how to get there and he issued left-this and right-that's until Dad turned the corner and we had a clear view of the field.

The view from the top of the hill of Grace A. Green Field was breathtaking. Both the varsity squad and freshman team shared the same practice grounds. I didn't have time to marvel. My heart was pounding. Sweat ran down the side of my face. I worried I'd have a repeat of the Chains of Rap Brown incident and have to walk onto the field with piss trickling down my legs while my testosterone-filled fellow freshmen leered at me and laughed. But I wasn't about to tell my dad the truth. If I'd come clean, he'd have beat the black off my butt, as he sometimes so eloquently put it.

Before the wheels on Dad's car came to a complete stop, I jumped out with my never-before-used practice clothes in hand and charged down the hill toward the only familiar face I knew, Coach Russo.

When I arrived, totally out of breath, sweating from my downhill run (proving what "great" conditioning I had from all my accumulated days of nonexistent training), it seemed to me as if Coach Russo towered over me, even though I had an inch or two on him.

Faced with the fear of being caught lying, I began to beg and plead, "Please! Coach Russo, I told my father I was on your team even though I knew I wasn't. He's gonna kill me if he finds out I was lying to him. Please! I'll do anything you say, if you'll just let me play on your team." Right after the words flew out of my mouth, my heart stopped racing. Just as my grandmother always said it would, the truth was setting me free.

Until that moment, I thought the tiny – and not so tiny – ways I twisted the truth, would only affect me. Standing there, waiting for Coach Russo to respond, I recognized that what I said and did had an impact. I had compromised the values I'd been taught, and, despite my fear, I was ready to accept whatever happened next.

Coach Russo looked past me up the hill to where my dad and Mr. Williams were standing. I braced myself, but instead of outing me, the coach waved. Then, he put his whistle to his lips and blew. "Go join your team, McLemore," he ordered.

He blew the whistle again. I hurried over to join the other congregating freshmen. I didn't know yet that the group I was joining was made up of young men who would soon become my closest friends, or that the team would be responsible for my fondest teenage memories, and for forever changing the trajectory of my life.

I knew nothing about football, yet, when the mighty whistle blew, I dropped to the earth and began doing push-ups (They actually called them up-downs), along with everybody else. Without ever explicitly saying it, Coach Russo taught me that an essential part of character was to be willing to take action, even in the face of fear.

I looked up at the top of the hill. There was my dad, standing tall on the hillside of Grace A. Green, watching me, his son, play a game he'd always called stupid. Until the day my father passed away, he would occasionally reminisce about his pride at watching his boy Kevin play a man's game. He never knew about my lie. No one told him. Coach Russo believed he could make an impact on my life by giving me a chance to make things right.

A couple of years ago, I was on a subway in New York City when I noticed a pretty, well-built lady stepping onto the train. Anyone with eyes in his head could tell she invested a great deal of time and energy into her appearance. But what caught my eye wasn't her perfectly shaped body.

It was the T-shirt she wore, which yelled out to all that looked at her that she didn't come easy. On the front was a halftone picture of herself in a very revealing bathing suit. On the back, it read, *do not wish for what you're not willing to work for.*

Without knowing it, Coach Russo stood at the intersection of one of my life's crossroads, pointing me in the direction not merely of wishing, but of work. Up until then, I'd been telling myself I was entitled to more than I'd gotten out of life. I'd resisted expending any effort out of a misplaced sense of self-pity. I wasn't the first black kid to be abandoned by a parent, and I certainly wasn't the first kid to grow up poor.

I lined up on the sidelines with everyone else, dug down deep, mustered my resolve, and ran wind-sprint after wind-sprint. At some point during that practice, in between the alarm of Coach Russo's whistle, I made a commitment to myself that I would never let him down.

I was ready to do whatever it took to get my life right.

Lying to yourself defeats the lines of communication to your soul. Like clouds obscuring sunlight, it blocks your ability to see the goodness in yourself and others. On the other hand, if you can look yourself in the eyes and answer in your heart that you've been telling the whole truth and nothing but, you've done a great service to yourself, and those who are lucky enough to know you. Operating in that gray area, peppering your conversations with one excuse after another, perceiving that nothing is ever your fault, is the surest way to get cut from the team of life.

Not everyone is lucky enough to have a Coach Russo, someone who will stand for their success even when they're in the midst of failure.

After that day, I started telling the truth. After that day, I stopped pretending my mother was dead.

CHAPTER 3

ONCE IN A WHILE, EVERYONE SHOULD RUN A COUPLE OF WIND SPRINTS

Imagine standing on the one-yard line of a football field, clad in shorts and a T-shirt. There are four other people beside you, each of them also dressed in running gear. They look up the field. You look up the field. As much as you've just declared yourself a member of their team, you want to win, which means one of them will have to lose and the other two will end up in the middle, somewhere between mediocrity and greatness. Forty yards ahead is your goal. Your mission is to get there faster than anyone.

"Procrastination, is the first door to open to mediocrity."

"Get ready!"

Up to the hill, beyond the football field, Dad and Mr. Williams were still there, watching. I dug my foot deeper into the earth for better traction. The whistle hung loosely from Coach Russo's lips. The hairs on the back of my neck stood on end. I looked down the line to see if what burned in my heart burned as brightly in the hearts of my competitors.

I gave myself a little pep talk. *I'm going out and get what is rightfully mine. I got this!*

My competition left a beat before the signal. I waited until the whistle.

As soon as I heard it, my brain and body propelled me forward with a singleness of purpose I'd never experienced before – except on the night of the Chains of Rap Brown. I was just a couple of steps behind Mister Quick Start. My body felt as if it would explode. I held nothing back. Now, we were neck and neck. What edge he thought he'd get by cheating had been lost. I pulled ahead, crossing the finish line first.

I fell to the earth, exhausted. The whistle blew again, directing me to get ready for the next round. Each time out, we were expected to give 100 percent.

Wind sprints taught me the importance of being prepared at a moment's notice to do and be my best. They broke us down, yes, but with persistence and repetition, they built us up as well.

I've come to believe we all come into this world focused, true to our purpose, and built for speed. With time, we learn to be less. Wind sprints helped me get in touch with the toughness I hadn't realized was within me.

My Uncle Bill used to say, "A man who knows himself is no longer a fool, for he now stands on the feet of his own wisdom."

I learned a lot about myself running out there in that heat that day. The game was hard, especially as we tried to master our strengths and work to control our many weaknesses. Yet, we were all greater than our circumstances. We could've let fear, uncertainty, or exhaustion, get the better of us, but instead we toed up to the line, ran the next wind sprint, and never allowed ourselves to stop to question whether we could do it.

Football taught me that we should concentrate on what we can do in life, not on what we can't. Then, as soon as our intentions are clear, all that's left is to dig our feet deep into the earth, wait for the whistle to blow, and run as many wind sprints as we can stand – even if you are lined up next to Mister or Miss Quick Start.

CHAPTER 4

THE GREAT ONES STAND
FOR SOMETHING

"You can learn more about a man in an hour of play than a year of conversation."

-Plato

In my old neighborhood, there used to be a saying: *Put up or shut up.* The ones that put up were respected and feared. The ones that shut up got the crap beat out of them for not standing up for themselves. Or – and this was far worse – they went on to live a life of shame, with their cowardice being replayed at every social gathering.

"Remember that time you punked out, Man?"

"Damn. You could've stood up for yourself, but instead you did nothing."

I learned early on that people would be evaluated based on whether they were willing to take action, especially action toward a purpose they believed in.

Long before I ever got to high school, I was one of a few underprivileged children who attended the local boys' club when the greatest man of our time paid us a visit. When that month's issue of *Life* magazine came out, I was on the cover of it along with a half dozen other kids, all of us clustered around the greatest man in sports – Muhammad Ali, aka "The GOAT."

Muhammad Ali came along during the sixties, when whites didn't like blacks, Jim Crow was law, blacks were dying for equal rights, women had to fight for access to the work place, and the Vietnam War was in full swing, despite all the protesting against it.

At a press conference, with the threat of being stripped of his title and sent to jail if he didn't serve his country, Muhammed Ali was asked why he would be willing to give up all that he had, including his freedom, rather than serve his country.

The boxer looked the reporter who'd asked the question right in the eyes. Then, he asked a question of his own: "Why should I go and fight people? Those people never did anything to me."

No matter how heavy the price, Ali stood behind his beliefs. As far as he was concerned, there was no gray area or in-between. Since he was willing to exist in absolutes, so was everyone around him. People either loved or hated him. But everybody, even the men he beat in the ring, respected that he had strongly held convictions and wasn't afraid to let his point of view be known.

I believe that it was his steadfastness that enabled Ali to achieve something no man had ever done before, unless you consider Jesus, who I believe was God and not merely a man.

For most, time is relentless. It doesn't let us go back. But Ali said he'd come back, and he did.

The second time I saw Muhammad Ali, I sat in one of the best seats in the house at Radio City Music Hall. My good friend Carole Rosen, a film producer at HBO, had given me a ticket to attend as her plus-one where we watched the living legend walk among a sea of people to approach center stage. Everything seemed to be happening so fast and, at the same time, occurring in slow motion. Actor Danny Glover introduced him, then, one by one, every person in the amphitheater came to their feet, where we remained standing and applauding for nearly twenty minutes. I looked around and saw people from all walks of life and every corner of the globe honoring a man who'd held true to his cause.

Ali was the embodiment of a lesson I'd learned from Coach Russo. The difference between winners and losers is that winners do the things losers don't have the courage to do.

I made it through my first day of practice without Dad or Mr. Williams ever catching on, but that didn't make the days that followed any easier. Less terrifying, sure, yet more demanding than anything I'd ever done. It felt as if all we ever did was run wind sprints. But wind sprints were part of the program, and following the program was what it took to win. That wasn't to say it was completely monotonous. Coach Russo had taken us from running on the field to running up the hill. This new approach was considerably harder, but he told us that, if we trained tough, when game time came, it'd all pay off.

It was hot. Really hot. No breeze, just heat. After running ten of these almost-unbearable saunas-temperature wind sprints, one of my teammates, Randy, dropped to his knees and refused to keep going. Coach Russo encouraged him to continue at a slower pace. Randy refused. He said he'd had enough. There was nothing anyone could say that would make him sprint another sprint. Coach pulled him to the side. I couldn't hear the whispered words of their exchange, but by the time Coach Russo blew his whistle for us to line up again, Randy was walking down the hill, in the direction of the locker room.

Coach Russo addressed the rest of us. "Progress is the result of taking an unpopular position. It comes from never giving up." He placed the whistle back in his mouth, where it dangled like a talisman. "Football isn't for everyone, and neither is life. Now line up!"

My legs screamed, my heart pounded, and my tongue felt like a dry towel left out in the sun, but, as soon as Coach Russo blew his mighty whistle, I charged up the hill with all the speed I could summon. Now, more than ever, I was determined not to let him down.

CHAPTER 5

"ARE YOU WILLING TO DO WHAT IT TAKES TO MAKE THE TEAM?" (THE UNIVERSAL QUESTION)

Do not wish for what you're not willing to work for, said the back of the shirt of the young lady on the subway train. The sentiment made me smile. These days, it seems as if everybody wishes for something more than they currently have, be it a better paying job, improved grades, better health, a stronger relationship, a slimmer waistline, a more cohesive family, an expanded network of friends… The list goes on and on. The real question isn't *What do you want?*, but *Are you willing to do whatever it takes to extricate yourself from the cycles that entrap you and keep you in whatever patterns of old behavior prevent you from committing to the choices that would enable you to achieve the life you say you want?*

As Randy walked toward the locker room to pack his gear and go home, I wished he'd have found the resolve to stick it out. Our coach wasn't requiring him to be the best, only to try his best each time out. When times get tough, we all want to quit, but life doesn't reward those who give up. Football was teaching me to keep moving forward. No matter what, keep moving forward. Whenever I thought I'd mastered a new skill, the coaches came up with a new drill that would make things even tougher. I was pretty sure they were trying to weed out those who said they wanted to be winners, but who weren't willing to make the sacrifices needed to earn the necessary W's. As for those of us who were willing to do whatever it took, we needed to push ourselves beyond our current capacity. The coaches recognized that. One windy afternoon, just before the end of that day's practice, the shrill whistle of Coach Montgomery, the head coach of the varsity squad, beckoned all of us – varsity, the reserves, and freshmen – to come together. Mostly, during the week, we freshman were segregated from the varsity squad, but sometimes on the weekends Coach Russo would have us join them for some of the less complicated drills. With the wind blowing to the north and the dirt in the middle of the field whirling around, we had been charging back and forth for hours, each time forming a small twister that seemed to billow up around us.

Coach Tom Montgomery stood in the middle of the field, like Mosses parting the Red Sea. The dirt didn't touch him. Standing by Coach Montgomery's side was his assistant coach, Coach Clemens and our very own Coach Russo.

My freshmen teammates and I stood in the middle of the dust bowl, shoulder-to-shoulder with the guys we'd only ever worshipped from a distance. The varsity team consisted of strong, battle-hardened warriors. We were a bunch of boys, waiting our turn to be men.

Coach Montgomery (nicknamed Groundhog from the days when he himself played football) had this expression that we could hear from the other side of the practice field. Whether he was raging mad about something gone wrong, or praising a player for a well-executed play, "Shit fire!" seemed to be his instinctive response. We'd hear the words echo through the air. He said them now before directing us to form a circle, with him in the center.

"Shit fire!" he bellowed. "Roosevelt High School is an institution! On this field, I'm that institution! We are the Mighty Fighting Teddies, and, even though you are on this team, a part of you wants to be your own person. You may feel the need to drink or use drugs, smoke, disrespect your mother or your girlfriend, or conduct yourself in ways that are socially unacceptable, or even unlawful. If that kind of behavior is okay by you, you have no place here. If you're on this team, you are a part of a 'We' system. 'We' don't do drugs, drink, or smoke. 'We' don't abuse or disrespect women. We don't lie, steal, cheat or any do any other destructive behavior you can think of. If you decide you want to stay and be a part of this great institution, you had better be prepared to play this game the way life is played - hard."

Even in the distance, the dirt stopped dancing.

"When we get knocked down, not only do we fall forward, we jump right up. If you lay there too long, it gets hard as hell to find a hand to pull you back to your feet. We win by being a team. There are no 'I's' in team. If 'I' wants to be a teddy, 'I' might as well quit now. We intend to beat the crap out of 'I'. In fact, if you want to see what a Mighty Teddy does to 'team I,' buy a ticket to one of our games and watch 'we' beat the crap out of 'I'!"

I wouldn't have thought it possible, but he got even louder. "A player on this team has the courage to do what he must for the betterment of the team, be it on the bench, in the game, or in life. When you wear the colors of this institution and you compromise your conviction, you compromise this program. When you make this program look bad, you'll have to deal with me. If you aren't true to your convictions, or your teammates, then this system will break you. Have the courage of your convictions, a commitment to excellence, and the guts to avoid anything that stands in the way of you becoming the best you that you can be!"

He pointed to the big guys – the varsity players – before turning to address his next comments to us lowly freshmen. "Four years ago, these guys were exactly where you are, and I stood in the middle of this field and made the exact same speech. Football has its setbacks; so, does life. We may not always win the game, but the scoreboard isn't always an indication of your worth. The universal question is, 'Are you willing to do whatever it takes to make this team?'"

Coach Montgomery blew his mighty whistle again, cueing the north wind that it was safe to start blowing again. This time, I refused to let my vision be obscured by the dirt. My attention was fixed on the big guys in the nice practice jerseys. Had they once been like me?

I envisioned myself as a towering senior, glaring at a group of lowly freshmen as Coach Montgomery talked about what it took to be a winner, and I resolved to do whatever it took to one day make the varsity team.

CHAPTER 6

PUT UP OR SHUT UP

After nearly two weeks of running wind sprints, jumping over old tires, pushing around an iron sled (on which Coach Russo caught a free ride... just because), my entire body hurt. No matter what direction I attempted to move, the pain was unbearable. I lay on my backside, staring up at nothing. My mind and body were in a state of conflict. I was determined to be one of those oversized varsity guys, but, at present, weighing in at only 134 pounds and standing 5'10" tall on my tippy toes, I felt underdeveloped. As the son of a mother who'd abandoned him and a father who regularly abandoned himself in a bottle, I felt insignificant.

I lay on my bed, feeling like a cardboard cutout and struggling to convince my body to get out of bed and follow my dream. But the pain! Oh, the pain! To blink was an effort! Bringing a dream to life takes 24-hours-a-day, seven-day-a-week commitment.

In 1994, just after the birth of my first son, Alexander, I placed a small woven net in the shape of a spider's web over the headboard of his bed. The net, a dream catcher, was intended to act as a lifelong reminder. Each night, even before he had the capacity to understand language, I would tell him how important dreams are. I would tell him that he was the only person who could make his dreams come true, then I would kiss him and whisper that he was, is, and always will be, loved, not only by his mother and me, but by the rest of the world. He would cup his tiny hands, as if to confirm that his dreams were in his hands, and roll over into the fetal position, clasping his curled fists to his chest. My infant son found a way to protect his dreams. He held them close to himself. Most people aren't willing to invest the amount of time and effort that's needed to manifest their heart's desires.

I didn't learn that vision without effort is useless until I learned to play football. The coaches told us repeatedly that to be a Mighty Teddy was going to take a lot of hard work. They hammered home the reality that wanting something was only part of the equation. We had to be willing to do whatever it took to position ourselves for success.

At fourteen years of age, I knew what I wanted. At 134 pounds, I knew I needed an edge. I managed to get myself up and out of my bed at four o'clock each morning, put on my freshman practice gear, and head outside for some self-inflicted wind sprints. I ran each wind sprint all out, uphill, with a flashlight in my hand. If I was going to make the varsity team, I needed to get in the best shape I could. If it meant one day wearing one of those nice practice jerseys, whatever personal sacrifices my dreams demanded would be worth it.

CHAPTER 7

DOING WHAT MATTERS IS ULTIMATELY THE GOAL

"Doing what matters, ultimately, is the goal in life," Uncle Bill said. "Writing down what matters, makes it a matter of fact."

I started writing in a journal freshman year of high school, after attending a speaking engagement in which Napoleon Hill addressed a group of us students. "Make notes and take notes," he instructed. From that moment onward, I did. My written words became a mirror of who I was and who I was becoming. Every time I wrote down what was happening or how I was feeling, it enabled me to look at my situation with at least a measure of objectivity and distance, which enabled me to assess myself, make changes, and take ownership of the impact my actions were having on the results in my life.

Memorializing memories also allowed me to review what I had written and see things I might never have seen without such an invaluable tool for self-assessment. Even though I might not have always liked what I saw reflected in the mirror of my journal, this kind of "retro-discovery" was a propeller, pushing me forward.

I've kept each and every one of my journals, which span a period of more than forty-five years. There are too many to count. When it came time to capture experiences so I could relay them in this book, my journals proved an invaluable resource. I didn't have to recreate anything. All I had to do was take what I already had and utilize it as best I could – yet another skillset for which football had prepared me.

Before I became acquainted with Coach Russo, Coach Clemens, and Coach Montgomery's philosophies, I had no answers and no plan. The system to which I subscribed was *Whatever happens, happens. I'll deal with it as it comes.*

They taught me that to fail at life, we have to create a formula for failure. Likewise, to succeed, we need a formula. Everything in our lives – every circumstance, every situation, every relationship, every challenge – has one common denominator: us. We are the reason things either do or don't work out. This can be a painful pill to swallow, especially as a parent.

In 1998, I received an invitation to visit my daughter's high school. The invitation wasn't the kind I'd have hoped for. My child wasn't receiving an award for outstanding achievement, which would have given me a lifetime of bragging rights. It was the other kind of call, the kind that confirmed what everyone else was saying, that I wasn't all that. My kid just proved it.

My oldest daughter, the product of a forgotten relationship, was, sadly, a reflection of the views I'd grown up with. Pops may have valued hard work and education, and read more books than anyone I ever knew, but in our family, we erected glass ceilings for ourselves when it came to the realm of higher education. The message I'd unwittingly passed down to my daughter was that, when it came to school, all she had to do was do well enough to get into a halfway decent college. I figured she would graduate from a second-rate school, find a job that made her happy (and made her enough money to pay her own bills), find a guy I halfway liked, get married, and have a kid or two. I fantasied that she would tell her kids – my grandkids – what a great dad I was, and how lucky they were to have me as the family patriarch. That way, when I traveled westward from the East Coast once or twice a year to see them, they'd know what a profound impact I'd had on their lives.

Looking back now, my thought process was laughable. I'd failed to impart to my daughter the lessons of character, integrity, and rigor that Pops, Uncle Bill, my coaches, and my grandmother had instilled in me. I didn't think I had to.

Up until high school, my daughter had been a straight "A" student. She'd gotten a music scholarship to attend an exclusive music academy and demonstrated that she had the potential to lead a dynamic, purposeful life. She didn't end up going to the school. The logistics of getting her there proved too much for her mother to manage, so she attended Belmont High instead.

When I was growing up, Belmont High had been the "white school" but by the time my daughter got there it had become integrated and diverse. It had also become notorious for its students' poor performances and inadequate educational outcomes. Nevertheless, despite its reputation, I wasn't prepared for her declining scholastic achievement. Funny how I'd been all too willing to take ownership of her accolades yet acted surprised when my absence as a live-at-home father caught up with me in the form of her declining academic performance.

My Uncle Bill once said to me, "In high school, there is no reality, only perception."

The phone call from my daughter's high school counselor (who just happened to be one of the counselors at my high school back in the day), informing me that my daughter was not doing as well as I wanted her to alerted me to my misperceptions. I'm not saying I was solely to blame. Every conventionally conceived child has two parents who play a pivotal role in their early lives. The way each parent shows up – or doesn't show up – conveys powerful messages to an impressionable youngster. That doesn't mean that, no matter our parents' involvement, or lack thereof, each of us isn't ultimately responsible for determining the trajectory of our life. We are responsible for our circumstances. There's no denying that fact. Yet, there are some of us who are taught the tools of life early and often by the loving adults in their lives, and others who have to teach themselves and don't learn responsibility until later on in life – assuming they learn it at all.

I would like to believe it wasn't my daughter's original plan to be less than what was expected of her. Unfortunately, she fell into a "poor me," "I can't," "it's not my fault" attitude that colored the way she saw the world.

I flew from New York City, New York, to Dayton, Ohio to attend a week of high school alongside my daughter. (This is something I think every parent should do at least once with his or her children. If not for a week, then at least for a day). I walked the hallways of Belmont High School amidst baggy pants, dyed hair, body-piercings, tattoos, and tough guy attitudes with a pen in one hand and a notebook in the other, no doubt embarrassing my daughter, but I wanted to record as many details as possible in the hopes that maybe, just maybe, I could help her create a winning strategy that she might actually implement.

I couldn't figure out what had caused the sudden downturn in my child's life. I spent hours with her teachers, trying to hammer out the exact source of the problem.

Could it be that I was too far away? Was her poor performance a cry for help?

Even though I lived on the East Coast, I was always concerned about my daughter's well-being. "Daddy loves his little girl," I'd told her over and over again, forgetting that actions overpower words.

I knew deep down that, even if my being far away was part of the problem, it wasn't THE problem. My daughter's teachers all spoke highly of her. They told me they really liked her. This was not what I expected, considering that she was getting straight "D's" and "F's." I had her tested, to see if she had some sort of learning disorder. She didn't. Ironically, I did, although it wouldn't be discovered until many years later.

I was diagnosed with ADHD just before I turned 50. After my youngest daughter was diagnosed, I had myself tested. My oldest daughter did not have ADHD, or anything else that would've interfered with her capacity to learn. She passed each test with impressive marks. I spoke to her mother, who responded to my concerns by telling me flat out that there was nothing she could do.

"I have my own problems," she said. As if our daughter wasn't her responsibility.

I went back to my daughter's teachers and requested that they show me not just her overall grades, but individual grades for each of her assignments. Looking at what my daughter had done in the past and comparing it against her current performance, I discovered that there was one class (Art) where she was still doing well. She'd earned mostly "A's and "B's" on her class work.

When I asked her about Art class, her face lit up like a candle, and, to my surprise, when I asked if she'd mind if I spoke with her Art teacher, she took me by the hand then sprinted down the hall, with me right beside her, and made the introduction.

I felt like an idiot for not beginning with the Art teacher. She was the only one who had a clear perspective on the problem. Of course, she did, just as, when I was in high school, there were adults who saw the strengths and weaknesses in me. The Art teacher explained that my daughter would be passing all her classes if she would just come to school, pay attention and not fall asleep on the days she was there. I hadn't known she was falling asleep! During the week I was there, my daughter's weekly marks went from zeroes for not turning in her work, or F's for not turning it in on time, to A's and B's. She went from "I can't" to "It's done" and from "I forgot" to "Here's my homework."

This wasn't because of me. Not entirely, anyway. I didn't do her work for her. My presence simply made her hold herself accountable for the ramifications of her actions, something neither her mother nor I had been doing enough of.

I explained that, at the beginning of each school year, every student started out as an A student. To get anything less, they had to work at it. Consistent action with persistence is the formula to pursuing your goals. From the way I saw it, she'd worked hard at getting less. I tried to show her in one week what she could do if she chose to take control, turn in her work, stay awake, and happen to life rather than let life happen to her.

Bobby Knight, a famous college coach, once said, "Do what has to be done, when it has to be done, and as well as it can be done. Then do it that way all the time."

As surely as a formula works for winning, its inverse is guaranteed to lead to loss. When I'd been my daughter's age, I was determined not only not to lose, but to do whatever it took to be the ultimate winner.

I headed toward Coach Russo's office, still sore as all get out from the day's drills. With every step I took, my little legs, full of lactic acid, felt as weighted down as if I had been walking in waist-high mud.

My purpose in having a one-on-one with Coach was to discover what I needed to know what I needed to do to make the varsity squad. I wanted Coach to teach me the nuances of the game. Failure wasn't an option. In my mind, I was already wearing the jersey. I didn't want to wait my turn. I wanted to be a varsity player now, as a freshman.

In the words of my good friend, advertising executive and author John Emmerling, "If you really want something, before you can claim it, you have to tell somebody. And not just anybody. Tell someone who will hold you accountable."

So it was that, at 134 pounds, standing 5 foot 10 inches (including my mini-fro), I approached Coach Russo's tiny office and knocked with all the confidence I could conjure. Before the door opened, my body started to cramp from all the wind sprints, not to mention the extra workout I was doing at four a.m. each morning.

"Come in!" he barked.

I told Coach Russo that I knew I didn't have a clear understanding of the game, but I was willing to play wherever they felt I could be of most help to the team. Then, I thanked him for not turning me away the day my father and Mr. Williams brought me to the practice I'd had no right to attend. I gave him my word as a man that I would never let him down.

I was brought up to believe that a man's word was as good as a signature on a contract. Better. Growing up, Pops used to tell me that, back in his day, folks didn't need contracts for anything. Back then, he said, folks could be trusted. A handshake was a man's contract. I've taught my children the same thing, but I've added my own little twist.

"If a man can't stand by his word," I've told them too many times to count, "then, he stands alone, with nothing to stand for." Sometimes, when I'm feeling especially preachy, I'll add, "If you don't stand by your word, then the world will stand on you."

As I carefully laid out my plan, Coach Russo sat, silently, and listened. When I finished, he appraised me, then, speaking with his thick Sicilian accent, he replied, "You want to be on the varsity squad, huh? To be one of those guys, it's gonna take a lot of self-discipline. To be one of those guys is like a job. You must show up early and stay late. Even if you make it, to keep your place, you must be willing to work harder than the next guy. Treat practice like a real game, the big game. You understand me, McLemore?"

I nodded.

"You're going to have to work your butt off to improve your skills as a player and a leader. You've got God-given speed, and only He can take that away from you, but the work is up to you. If you do everything, I just told you, then maybe you can make the team. Not this year, but maybe next."

I didn't think he had heard what I said when I first entered his office. So, with respect, I corrected him. "I needed to know what I had to do to make the varsity team, Sir. My plan was this year."

"I told you what you need to know to make the team," he replied. "Become your own competition, and you'll be rewarded when the time is right. But, Kevin, this year is not realistic."

I'd made the decision to go to the next level and settled on the time frame in which I would do it. Now that Coach Russo had given me the steps, all I had to do was follow them.

To be successful at anything, you must have a well mapped-out plan. You don't have to spend every waking hour working toward your goal, but you need structure, flexibility, purpose, and the ability to infuse fun into the process.

I couldn't have articulated the importance of fun when I was in high school, pouring out my blood, sweat and tears to fuel my passion. Yet, it was surely there in the trash-talking, butt-slapping, joking and joviality, in the comradery between the players and the glint of approval in our coaches' eyes when we had done something to make them proud. The enjoyment was a byproduct of teamwork that I took for granted. It wasn't until later in life that I discovered that, if you're lit up by something you love, no matter how much time is required or how rigorous the requirements, it won't feel like work. Once I made this discovery, I started being intentional about incorporating fun into all my most "difficult" endeavors. It doesn't matter where you are in your life, be it a freshman in high school, a CEO of a large company, a professional risk taker, an entrepreneur, or a stay-at-home parent, to do what matters demands a tremendous amount of effort. But that doesn't mean life has to feel effortful. I know now that there are three essential forms of personal rigor that almost guarantee a person will reach his or her dreams: physical discipline, mental discipline, and spiritual discipline.

Ever since my high school days, I've been able to "make a good living, almost" (as my now ex-wife used to say) using physical discipline alone as the vehicle for arriving where I wanted to go. While I do believe that people who take care of themselves have a leg up, physical development is by no means enough. Mental discipline is also essential.

Each day, I devoted time to exercising my body and my intellect. I refused to limit my potential by drinking, using drugs or associating with less than genuine people. And I immersed myself in studying the game.

Coach Russo had rightly observed that God had given me the gift of speed. Not Lucinda Adams speed, but faster than a bullet being fired at me from the gun of the Chains of Rap Brown.

I am beyond grateful for my willingness to adhere to the message that Coach Montgomery issued the day when he stood like Moses in the center of a sea of dust and set forth his life-changing proclamation. He had made clear the importance of character. It was a lesson that, once learned, I never forgot.

As an adult, I had two friends, both of whom were chasing similar dreams only to find that something they did back in high school would shoot their dreams in the back, killing what mattered most to them without them ever seeing it coming. Just like that, Blam! Dream alive, now dead!

Both my friends were stand-up guys, leaders and productive, contributing citizens. One wanted to be an FBI agent, the other wanted to be a DEA agent. The friend that wanted to be an FBI agent spent three years going to law school at night while working the third shift as a doorman in an upscale New York high-rise on 79th street. The friend who wanted to work as a DEA agent had a full-time job as a health club manager and had custody of his five-year-old daughter. Both were ideal candidates for their desired future careers. Both had taken the necessary tests and passed at the top of their classes. But both got kicked out of their respective programs because, when asked if they had ever tried drugs, thinking that telling the truth would leave no question as to their characters, they answered truthfully. They had each tried drugs back when they were in high school, not thinking that what happened then would matter in the future. They were right there, the golden ring in reach, yet, because of something they did several decades earlier. Each was immediately disqualified from continuing on. Each was shattered. Their dreams were lost.

The earlier one starts to begin to prepare themselves for whatever it is they most want and the more committed they are to their vision, the better. This doesn't mean that people who've made mistakes can't learn from them and course correct. I've already confessed to how I nearly got gunned down by the Chains of Rap Brown, to lying about going out for football, and, before that, lying about the whereabouts of my mother.

The only difference between the friends who lost their dreams and me is that I had a purpose, given to me by football, and that I took it seriously enough to sacrifice immediate gratification for a long-term goal. I also had a journal.

It's important to write down what you want, what it's going to take to get there, then commit to your vision one hundred percent. Make note, take notes. Write down everything that happens that is worth remembering. Learn from each day's lessons. Revise your plan as you go, but stick to the vision you create for yourself and, even more importantly, be the person that attainment of that vision requires you to be.

My two friends are powerful examples of how being out of integrity with your dreams can cost you the opportunity to achieve them. No one is perfect, especially not me. I've made, and will continue to make, mistakes. But I do my best to make sure that the mistakes I make never cost me my dreams. And I thank God that, when I was still too young to understand how much my present actions would impact my future self, I made the decision to follow the directions of those older and wiser and more impressive than myself because who I am today, only came about from who I was trying to be when I didn't know who I was.

CHAPTER 8

―――――――――――――――――――――――――――――――――

TAKING THAT FIRST HIT

I jogged over to practice in the rain, dressed in my shorts and T-shirt, with my helmet in my hands. Coach Russo's words pressed against my brain as I entered the team locker room and was immediately assailed by the smell of Icy Hot. Nervous energy lingered in the air. Then, the big guys came in, all padded up in full gear, with their nice new practice jerseys and brand-new helmets. One by one, they filed into the room, roaring like mighty warriors preparing for battle. Some of them tossed their old smelly jerseys into the faces of us underclassman. Others ignored us entirely. Suddenly, ringing out over the mighty roar of those big guys, the voice of Coach Russo boomed out, calling his freshman squad over to the utility closet.

My teammates hurried over. I sat, unsure of what I was supposed to do. But then Phil Garrison (who we nicknamed Nick Hound because, back in the day, nicknames were a term of endearment (You didn't belong unless you got a nickname) slapped me dead center in the upper part of my back, nearly knocking my head off my shoulders.

"You best go get your stuff," he said.

I didn't know much about whatever the "stuff" was, but I figured I'd better get mine before the best of it was gone. I hurried over to the closet. Coach Clemens asked me what size I wore. I had no idea, but Coach Russo came to my rescue and handed me a pile. Back at my locker, more confused than I'd been before, I stared at the hodgepodge of oddly shaped items. The only thing I was familiar with was the helmet. What was I supposed to do with all the rest?

I soon learned that, just as a CEO wears a power suit, the gear I'd been given was the business suit of the Mighty Teddies. Sweat trickled down my forehead. I couldn't ask anyone what I was supposed to do. That would've revealed my ignorance and if I had any chance of making the varsity squad I had to seem as if I knew what I was doing. Luckily, I got help from a friend. A friend who'd been by my side many times before, a friend who ran with me at Westwood swimming pool the night the bullets were being fired at us from the guns of the Chains of Rap Brown.

After Jason showed me how to put my pads on, I ran down the hill, padded from head to toe – thigh pads, butt pads, kneepads; I had everything including a girdle. It was raining again. The sky was black. I figured that, because of the weather, we would practice for an hour at the most. I was wrong. Nothing stopped football.

Minutes later, lying there, stunned, my face planted in the mud with Big John Williams on top of me, I felt exhilarated. I never knew true fulfillment until I got knocked down. As I spit mud from my mouth and brushed away the mound of turf that was wedged in the corner of my face mask while waiting for him to separate his 220 pound frame from my little body, the voices of my coaches and teammates echoed through the ear holes of my helmet.

I got back on my feet. I had to overcome my lack of football knowledge. I had to figure out what to do next time to avoid another mud bath. I had to show my teammates as well as my coaches that I had what it took to play with the big guys.

When trying something new, it's natural to end up on your ass. What I learned on the football field was the same lesson I'd later learn about life: People can get by in the short run on raw talent, but in the grand scheme of things, only those who are in a constant state of self-improvement can expect to win. As the actor Will Smith says, "Being a realist is the most commonly traveled road to mediocrity."

A person who works on only the things they're good at will over-develop their strengths while their weaknesses become more exaggerated.

Giving up wasn't an option. I'd already resolved that I was making varsity. My lack of physical size was a deficiency, but I had been taught that people failed not because of their deficiencies but because of their inability to assess and overcome them, which usually resulted from a lack of self-reflection, or the absence of courage.

On that rainy day, the day when we got our gear, Coach Russo assigned me a position. "You're a middle guard, McLemore."

"Yes, sir, Coach." I didn't have a clue what a middle guard was.

My new stuff added 30 pounds to my existing 134. Big John had 30 extra pounds too, upping him from 220 to a solid quarter of a thousand.

I took my first hit, second, third, and so on. Each time I was knocked down, I got up, wiped the mud from my eyes, talked some trash, and went back for more. Then, Coach Russo called me over to the sideline. I thought he was going to take back the new equipment I'd only just gotten, tell me I was a disgrace, and send me home. Instead, he placed his arm around me. "You're doing a real good job out there, McLemore."

This confused the hell out of me. No matter how you sliced it, Big John was having his way. I was little more than a bug that he could not only subdue but squash. I stared at Coach, uncomprehending. He instructed me to go back on the field, line up, spit on the ground, and slap Big John upside his head as hard as I could, no matter if the ball was in play or not.

Before I returned to the huddle, still confused and now in fear for my life, Coach Russo said there was one more thing I needed to know. "You're faster than most of the guys out there. You're gonna slap him on the right side of his head as he faces you, which will knock him to your left. When you do that, you're going to open a hole on your right. Go to that open hole and knock the living hell out of anyone who shows up with a ball in his hand. Can you do that?"

"Yes, I can!"

I knew Coach Russo had my best interests at heart. If Big John were to kill me, Coach would get my body back home okay.

Dwight Anderson, our team's quarterback, "the G.O.A.T" called out the play. I freed my right hand from the mud, leaving it hanging as I began to wind up. I was fixed on Big John's head as he positioned the ball. Just as Dwight was hiking it, I slapped the right side of Big John's helmet, forcing his head and his big, muscular body to my left. The power of my slap and the way I timed the hit caused a missed connection between John and Dwight. The ball fell free from Dwight's hand, into the mud in front of me.

I jumped on the football. So, did everyone else.

"Fumble."

I was face down in the mud again. Only, this time, instead of Big John's, there were several other big, bulky bodies atop mine. When I finally got up and glanced over at the sideline, there was Coach Russo with an *I told you so* look on his face.

That day, I learned a lot of things. I learned that your body goes wherever your head goes. I learned that I could take a hit, multiple hits, and still retain the courage to risk it all. And, most important of all, I learned that, no matter how many times you find yourself face down, if a hundred Big Johns are lying on you, whoever comes up with the ball wins.

CHAPTER 9

MASTER IT, BY PRACTICING IT

With my God-given speed and Coach Russo's helmet-slapping strategy, I found my edge. As a matter of fact, my teammates christened me "the Black Ninja Head-Slapper." I got so slap-happy, I slapped stuff in my sleep.

At a whopping 134 pounds, I became the starting middle guard for the freshman Fighting Teddies. I even earned a spot on the suicide squad, "The Kickoff team" that the varsity used to practice their annihilation tactics. Nevertheless, I reminded myself to keep striving. Sure, lots of my fellow freshmen would've given anything for a starting position on the team, or a place on the suicide squad, but I wasn't content. Come to think of it, that's not true. Lots of my fellow freshmen wouldn't have given anything. They weren't running wind sprints outside of practice or knocking on Coach Russo's door. They were waiting for someone or something to inspire them. They were working only as hard as was required, whereas I was doing all I could to prepare myself in advance for whatever new challenges came my way. It's curious to me now that I had such a singleness of purpose in high school but, as an adult, I sometimes lost sight of my vision.

When my son, Alexander, was three, I was working on this book in a corner of the house I'd come to think of as my writing sanctuary. I'd been deep into the process for about an hour when I felt my little boy's eyes on me.

Alexander didn't say anything. He simply sat there, waiting. Yet, I experienced an overwhelming sense of pressure, as if he were willing me to turn around. I did. We made eye contact. He asked in the sweetest little voice if I would play with him. But, instead of putting my work down, I replied that I was working, and he had to wait. I was in the middle of a profound thought that I just had to get down on paper while it remained a fresh idea in my head. I gave him a quick kiss on his forehead, then, having just rejected a three-year-old, I turned back to my "important" work only to realize I'd forgotten what mattered. I'd become so fixated on putting in my two hours of writing a day that I separated myself from what was important.

For as long as I could remember, I'd wanted nothing more than to be the kind of father to my children that I wished I myself had had. I had promised I would be a better father to my children than mine was to me. But my relationship with my older daughter supported a different reality. I'd failed to practice consistent in-person availability. Sure, I had tried to be hands-on in her life, but living 1500 miles away, how available could I be? I made weekly calls, visited her school, sent money, and loved her from afar, but at my core I wished I'd done better. When push came to shove, I'd failed her.

To this day, one of my few regrets is that, despite loving her, I wasn't always there. Now, ten years later, here was Alexander. Football taught me that how you practice makes what you practice permanent. I had to start practicing good fatherhood. I refused not to show my son so much love that no one could ever claim I hadn't given fathering him my all.

CHAPTER 10

NOT EVERYONE PLAYS

For the first several weeks of the season, our status as Mighty Teddies remained distressingly uncertain. Coach Russo and Coach Clemens were continually thinning out the herd. Back in football's glory days, when the sport gave shape and substance to so many's lives, Sundays took shape around church and the game. There was no way I was going to let myself be one of the ones who got cut. I was too invested. Football had become everything to me. I had hustle and heart. All I needed was a better understanding of what I was supposed to be doing on the field and why I was supposed to be doing it.

At practice, I watched Jason Kirkland level anyone that came his way, with or without the ball. Simply observing my friend and ally in action taught me enough about the fundamentals of the game that I could start to play more strategically. Pretty soon, my repertoire had expanded beyond my patented head slap and I felt more assured that I was making contributions on the field. Not that anyone's spot was secure.

Well after my high school football days, after I moved to Phoenixville, PA, I saw a poster that read, *Team Sports Tryouts, Everyone Plays*. I didn't get it. Everyone played? Impossible. No matter how many ways the friend I was with tried to explain it to me, the concept didn't make sense. When a player is faced with daily incentives and stakes, knowing that even after they make the team, their status isn't assured, they develop intrinsic motivation. Or they demonstrate an unwillingness to try that would make them a detriment to a team if they'd been kept out of pity or "fairness."

What if billionaire Bill Gates sent out a press release that read, *we've decided that, at Microsoft, everyone who applies gets a job*? It would be as if, in taking that stance, he would be sending out the message *It's okay to be mediocre. We have no standards or expectations.*

In the September 1996 issue of the nationally circulated publication, *Advertising Age*, John Emmerling, Chairman of Emmerling and Post Advertising, sat down with Bill Gates to find

I find it ludicrous that there are supposedly "competitive" leagues out there today that give everyone equal time on the Asphalt. This practice is supposed to teach teamwork and improve self-esteem, but it seems to me that it strips the game of its grit and teaches players that performance doesn't matter. Why bother trying if the outcome will be the same either way?

Only the best Mighty Teddies got to play. The ones who were good, but not the best, either needed to push themselves to outperform those better than themselves, hope the best stopped excelling, or continue to strive enough to remain but not enough to make it out onto the field.

Everyone Plays thinking sabotages a system that has been created to keep the playing field from ever becoming equal. That doesn't mean I don't advocate for the underdog. I was a poor, scrappy black kid, growing up without a mother, trying to excel at football when he didn't even know the rules of the game. It's precisely because I was the underdog that I understand that, without the experience of giving everything I had to the impossible set of circumstances in front of me and triumphing over them and against my own doubts, fears and insecurities, I never would have come to believe in myself or to develop a process for achieving unprecedented results that I would carry with me for life.

If a person can successfully become their own competition, bet on their talent, and put their heart and soul into everything they do, they'll succeed.

My grandfather used to say, "Get knocked down seven times, get up eight, get up nine, get up ten." Just get up until you are so tired of getting knock down no one can knock you off whatever you want to do."

That's what I did. Over and over again, I got knocked down. Big John sat on me so often I was convinced I was at risk of developing a permanent imprint of his butt on my back. But each time I got back up having learned a lesson and with a newfound resolve. Nothing was going to stand in the way of my greatness.

HAPPINESS IS AN INSIDE JOB

"Through life people will upset you, disrespect you, treat you bad, try to make you feel bad about your success. Don't let hate in your heart consume you too, leave it to God to take care off."

Charles Darwin

I was baffled by Kelli Spicer. Each day, he would come to practice and get the living crap kicked out of him, and, as far as I can remember, he never played in a single game, yet he never complained. His smile was relentless. No matter what people said, or did, to him, he only ever had good things to say about other people.

In 1993, when the movie "Rudy" came out, watching it was like watching Kelli Spicer's life projected on a big screen. In the film, the main character, Rudy, is born into a blue-collar family. Rudy's prospects are limited and his problems are many. Despite this, however, and even though his life path seems to have been predetermined for him, Rudy is determined not to end up working in the steel mills alongside his father and brothers. He dreams of going to Notre Dame and playing for famed coach Ara Parseghian and the Fighting Irish. Like Don, Rudy wasn't big enough or fast enough, but nothing was going to stand between him and his dreams. Some might describe me as a Rudy of sorts, but this wouldn't be accurate. I worked hard, yes, but I started with a natural athletic aptitude and I had friends like Jason Kirkland who helped me fill in the knowledge gaps between what I didn't know and what I needed to.

Kelli Spicer was a living testament to the power and triumph of a common man. He began at a distinct disadvantage, yet he played with the most heart of anyone I ever knew. He earned his spot on the team. His willingness to give his all to every drill, and at every practice, even when it was clear he wouldn't see any playing time in games, taught me a lot about the importance of contribution.

Kelli Spicer was eager to add value in any way he could. He came to practice early, stayed late, gave his all, got flattened, got up, then gave his all again. This willingness to dig deep, work hard, and seemingly come up short made him an invaluable asset. We all loved Kelli Spicer. He added immensely to the cohesion of the team, proving that attitude is as important as action. His passion and positivity weren't just relegated to the football field, either. When football season ended, Kelli Spicer and I ran track together. He was far from the fastest, but he ran harder and put more of himself into each race than anyone else. Plus, when it wasn't his turn to run, he cheered so loudly from the sidelines that his enthusiasm propelled us, his teammates, forward.

I don't know where or what Kelli Spicer is doing today, but if he is the same Kelli Spicer, I played football and ran track with, I am certain he's living a happy, fulfilling life.

I cannot overstate the impact playing with him had on me, then or now.

Years ago, while I was still in high school, I had the pleasure of coaching an age group summer track club. I wasn't too far removed from being a child myself, but since I was an athlete fast approaching becoming my own man, coaching was a natural position for me. Because of my youth, it was easy to show young people what I wanted from them. Instead of having to stop at explanations, I could demonstrate. I could teach by example, rather than by lecture.

The kids I was assigned to work with had a lot of potential. They ran hard and they were coachable. Yet, because the team had been functioning more as a track club than a competitive, organized group of athletes for years, most of the teams we faced off against never thought of us as competition. We never had been before.

The Mighty Teddies were winners by tradition, so I had some personal adjusting I had to do to work with developing young minds and to straddle the line between enjoyment and excellence. I began to look over the talent I'd been assigned to work with and started to place my players where I thought they would be most competitive. My goal was to foster their love for the sport rather than to wipe the floor with our competitors. We developed a mind-set that, if we functioned as a team, we'd already won. I encouraged them to give 110% of themselves, win or lose, and to have fun. This soon became our team motto: 110%, no matter what the place. What happened next was nothing short of miraculous. Every one of my athletes began to run as if they believed they could win.

As the summer track season was winding down, some of our standout kids qualified for an invitational meet that was being held in Chicago. There was also an open registration for the age group, where anyone in the age group could run the race of his or her choice. We took as many of our kids as could afford to go. Only, when we got there, we discovered that the open registration ranged from ages 8-10, 12-14 and 15-17. This pleased all but one of our kids.

Little Kelly happened to be six. There was no group for her to run in. Before the Chicago meet, Kelly had always been able to compete, but the meet officials had opted not to run a 4-6 age group. They didn't want to prolong the meet by running events for younger kids who took longer to finish and generally required greater supervision. To protest Kelly's exclusion from the meet, Kelly's parents and I filed a formal complaint, which, under the rules, had to be addressed immediately. Not in writing, either. We opted to meet face-to-face with the officials and to address our concerns about their policy head-on. They were so taken-aback by our brazenness that they didn't even put up a fight. They immediately agreed to give Kelly the chance to run in the open events, but there was another problem, they pointed out, which had to be addressed.

Kelly was the only 6-year-old registered at the meet. She couldn't run against her peers. The race officials opted to let Kelly run with the 8-10-year olds and said they'd give her a trophy if she finished the race, regardless of her place. We returned to Kelly to tell her she could participate! We told her to finish the race and give 110% for her effort. We didn't disclose that she'd win a prize irrespective of her place at the end of the race. We wanted it to be a surprise, but, when she informed us that she wanted to run the open mile with the 8-to-10-year olds, our previous exuberance was replaced by apprehension. I worried that a mile-long race would be too long, and she wouldn't finish and would end up not getting a trophy. As her coach, I felt responsible for setting her up to succeed, so I tried to get her to try another race. One she might be more successful in, like the one-hundred-yard dash (a race she had run all summer).

When I explained that a mile was four very long laps around the very big track, she informed me matter-of-factly that the mile was the race she wanted to run. Her parents were crushed. At age six, matched against girls two to four years older and exponentially more developed, Kelly was taking on a personal challenge none of us thought she could meet.

In the spirit of the game, and, I thought, against my better judgment, we let Kelly have her way. We'd fought to let her run. We owed it to her to let her compete in an event of her choosing. Kelly's mother pinned her number to her little jersey, and I walked her to the track where the 8-to-10-year olds were warming up. Sizing up Kelly's competition, it was clear that my tiny racer was outmatched. Surely, she'd finish dead last – if she finished at all.

The gun aimed high in the air. The shot rang out loud. Smoke from the starter pistol cleared as the 8-to-10-year olds took off for a mile run, with six-year-old Kelly pulling up from the rear. I held tight to the rail near the stands. Kelly's parents held on too. The other spectators cheered for little Kelly as she made her way around the track. She was so cute, her blonde ponytail bouncing as her little legs worked overtime. Just as the racers were making their way into the third lap, some of the older girls began to slow down. Others came to a stop, opting to drop out, bested by the length of the race they themselves had chosen to run. Not Kelly. She had moved from last to fifth place. She was in the race now. By the time she entered the final lap, she had advanced two more positions.

At the 110-yard mark, with her little legs moving twice as fast as the others, Kelly caught up to the leader. She pulled ahead. Now, she was in the lead! The crowd came to their feet as the announcer gave the play-by-play of the finish, and little Kelly put some serous distance between herself and all the other runners, who were trailing after her.

Running across the finish line, Kelly set a record in a race where I thought she wouldn't finish, let alone place. With the first-place trophy in hand, a prize she'd earned and not simply been given, she made her way through the stands with tears of joy in her eyes, jumped into my arms, and yelled, "Coach, I broke the tape! I broke the tape!"

Turns out, Kelly's goal hadn't been to win. She simply wanted to be the one who broke the tape. It never dawned on her that she'd overcome a major obstacle. I don't know why breaking the tape was so important to her any more than I know why being one of the big guys was once so important to me.

In my entire coaching career, there has been no greater moment in my life as a coach than the day I watched Kelly cross the finish line and break the tape. Any limitations she faced were not her own, but were set by people who thought they had her best interests at heart by encouraging her not to try what they thought was impossible. It shames me to admit that I was almost a dream stealer. I taught the kids I coached to be competitors, take on challenges, and fling open the doors to unlimited possibility. Kelly taught me the importance of standing for a vision, even when the achievement of it might seem impossible. I count my blessings for the lessons in life that were taught to me by six-year-old Kelly and the original team player, Kelli Spicer. Sometimes, when I'm bumping up against real or imagined obstacles, I remind myself to take a deep breath, think with my heart instead of my head, look at what's really important, embrace the moment, and, against what I believe to be my better judgment, pick the race I want to run most, even if winning seems unlikely.

Thinking back on Kelly's victory, I'm reminded of how much resolve matters. Words matter. Kelly set out with one purpose in mind – breaking the tape. She ignored her naysayers (me among them), focused on the desire within, set a pace, and stuck to it.

In sharing what it felt like to break the tape, Kelly reminded me how impactful resolve can be. She declared that she would run. She believed in herself, then made happen exactly what she wanted to have happen. Whatever the outcome of the race that day, her willingness to compete against all odds made her a winner even before she broke the tape. Her experience reminded me of my own experience freshman year when Coach Russo outlined the formula for success while simultaneously making clear that it would take time for me to achieve it. I didn't have to wonder if he'd felt about me the way I felt about Kelly. I already knew the answer.

CHAPTER 12

REAL FAITH LASTS A LIFETIME

"What we call the beginning is often the end. To make an end is to make a beginning. The end is where we start from."

-T.S. Elliott

I was determined to become one of the guys on the varsity team. Never mind the obstacles.

I ran wind sprints harder, did pushups harder, and slapped Big John's head harder than anyone else on the field. He, in turn, knocked me on my butt. It barely fazed me. I was a young man on a mission. I never even contemplated uttering the words "I quit." Determination, heart, hustle, and my willingness to learn netted me five extra pounds and the starting middle guard position. Number 64, down on the front line with the big boys, dead center, right in the middle of the action. In the first three games of our season, I scored two defensive touchdowns on fumbles, blocked one punt, and had one interception. I wasn't as big as most of the players I faced, but I was faster. Plus, I'd mastered the head-slap.

When the game was at its toughest, I played my best. I liked a good fight. As a matter of fact, I still like a good fight. I'm not talking about fist fights. I'm talking about opportunities for growth through struggle.

Experience has taught me that the more you're challenged, the more alive you have the capacity to feel – if you use those challenges to your advantage, rather than allowing yourself to be used by them.

Too many people have a "plan A" and a "plan B." I don't entertain the ideas of B-plans. I throw myself wholeheartedly at my first choice, then I brace myself for what's to come. I learned that from Uncle Bill, who always said that anything other than your "A" plan is a distraction. Dreams become realities only when we align powerfully behind them and move forward with inspiration and perspiration. I put my faith in positive living and thinking, hard work and perseverance. And I have unshakeable faith.

J.F. Clark wrote, "All the strengths and forces of men and women come from their faith in the things unseen. He who believes is strong; he who doubts is weak. Strong conviction precedes great action."

In my lifetime, I've seen and heard a lot of things. I have witnessed people taking their last breaths or horribly injured and each time these stalwart nonbelievers called on something beyond themselves for help and solace at the moment when they knew they were beyond all human aid. With every man or woman who has claimed he didn't believe in God, or any other spiritual being, in times of great pain or shortcomings, whom do you think he or she calls on?

Before every game, the team would gather around the coaches and pray for the safety of our teammates, as well as the safety of our opponents. But even though when the coach led us in prayer, he was clear about wanting safety and well-being for our adversaries, he would ask for victory for us.

Some people might not understand this time-honored tradition of sports teams praying to win.

"If you pray, and your opponents pray, won't your prayers just cancel each other out?" they want to know. They don't understand that prayer is only the beginning. Winners set a powerful intention, speak it out into the universe, then apply everything they've got to realizing what it is they want.

In my experience, hard work without intentionality isn't enough. In order to achieve great things, one must have a reason – a why.

CHAPTER 13

A PRELUDE TO LIVING LIFE WELL IS TO LIVE IT WITH AN ATTITUDE

The more time I put into practicing the game of football, the better I got. Walking out onto Grace A. Green field as a freshman, I was only a small reflection of the man I would eventually become, but I was starting to develop the mindset of someone who knew deep down in his gut that he could make anything possible.

Attitude and action are the key elements that separate the winners from the losers. This doesn't mean that winners never suffer short-term losses. In my personal quest to make the varsity team, I got knocked on my butt plenty of times. I looked at each of these experiences as a means to an end, and I kept developing my skillset such that I became increasingly prepared for the next opportunity. Successful people don't just want to win. They expect to win. They get a taste of what it's like, and they want to repeat that feeling again and again. I went into game situations expecting to be the victor and nothing less. I believe that a person who is in good physical condition and lives a life with a "can do" attitude can out-perform almost anyone.

I developed tunnel vision for the end zone. The first time I picked up a loose ball, fumbled by the other team's quarterback, I ran that baby in for a touchdown. Every time thereafter, if I got my hands on a loose ball, I intended to score.

My end-zone-only philosophy of life set me apart from my more tentative teammates and caught the attention of the varsity football coach, Coach Montgomery. Unbeknownst to me, the coaches had all been talking and Coach Montgomery had asked Coach Russo if I could practice with the varsity special team. Of course, Coach Russo said "yes," and soon enough I was splitting my practice time between the freshman squad and the varsity special team. The varsity guys ran faster, hit harder, and had faster reflexes, which meant they were much harder to hit with my patented head-slap. It didn't matter. Everything was working as planned. Or that's what I thought, until my first day on the special team. What I quickly discovered was that being among the big guys wasn't going to be the prestigious position I'd envisioned.

As I made my way down the field, being pushed around like a rag doll, there was laughter over on the sidelines from some of the heroes I'd been admiring from afar. I joined the rest of the special team on the sideline.

"Welcome to the squad," one of my towering teammates said.

The whistle beckoned shrilly, and I hurried out onto the field. At that time, in Dayton, Ohio, football was more than a recreational pastime. It was a way of life. We had over 100 kids come out for the team. Those that made the starting squad were the best of the best. The second stringers were good enough that they could've been starters at almost any other school. The special team, aka the "suicide squad," was the kickoff team. Those of us who'd made it onto the suicide squad were expendable. We ran full speed ahead with reckless abandon, tasked with one critical mission – to knock the crap out of anyone who had the ball. This also meant we routinely got the crap knocked out of us.

To say I got the brunt of it would be an understatement, yet I put my helmeted head down and tried even harder. After all, I was one step closer to what I wanted to be, a few less yards away from my intended end zone.

My resolve was stronger than ever. I would wear the Mighty Teddy varsity jersey. I didn't care whether I made it into a game or remained seated proudly on the bench. The suicide squad was only a beginning. My goal was to be a recognized member of the team by the end of the season, which meant I had five more weeks in which to achieve the thing that mattered most.

CHAPTER 14

THE BULL IN THE MIDDLE

Like Coach Russo, Coach Montgomery was the kind of man who always thought five plays ahead. The more I was around him, the more I understood the Robert Collier quote: "Success is the sum of small efforts – repeated day in and day out."

The suicide squad was a promotion. I still had my full-time duties as the starting middle guard on the freshman squad, and I got to get the crap kicked out of me by the big guys on varsity. But it wasn't enough to work toward a secret, unarticulated goal.

I believe I got the suicide squad promotion because I told somebody what I wanted, and that person went on to tell another person, and, while those two people, who knew what I wanted, were deciding whether or not to take a chance on me, I was doing all the things I needed to do to get to where I wanted to be. They saw that and rewarded me accordingly. In this case, accordingly wasn't just promising. It was painful. My job was to blindly hurl myself onto another human being and put enough of a hurting on him that he'd wish he were never born, and Coach Montgomery would see my potential, while his job was to put the same hurting on me.

There were eleven guys on each side of the field, all trying to get Coach Tom Montgomery's attention, and one guy waiting in the wings. He'd already done his part by kicking the ball.

Having the opportunity to practice with the varsity squad made a major difference in my abilities. As freshmen, we were developing skills, but those big guys already knew what they were doing. Varsity players played the game on a whole other level! They'd achieved aptitude and were well on their way to mastery.

The Powell twins' eyes could burn a hole right through you. Big Larry Hightower, the team's star running back, ran the ball through holes in the line like an unstoppable train. Herd Smith, the team's option quarterback, was smooth as silk as he stood behind the center and read the defense. Without them ever knowing what he was up to, he could assess them perfectly, knowing what each of them was about to do, and when they were going to do it, with clarity and surety.

Each member of our starting squad was an unstoppable force. Never once did any of them show the slightest bit of apprehension. They were one big, mighty, hurting, fighting machine, charging down the field. They gave their all on every play, play after play, after play. Watching their example, I learned that to operate on the level of a champion, you must work within and with "The System" while behaving as if greatness is a foregone conclusion.

It's a shame that, in our day-to-day lives, most people don't strive for success the way football teams do. Wouldn't it be nice if during life's many situations, everybody looked out for each other and worked together toward one unified cause? In the world we live in today, there are a lot of people who talk about "being a team player," but, when examining their behaviors, it seems clear that they're operating from a perspective of *me first, then me again, then you, if and only if I feel like it, which I probably won't,* basis.

If you take a hard look at the corporate system, there are a lot of parallels between sports teams and big businesses. The owner is the CEO, President or General Manager. Then, you have the person who oversees the day-to-day operations, who could be likened to a coach. His or her job is to call down the plays to an assistant, or manager, who then has to see to it that the workers, i.e. the players (the running backs, tight ends, linemen, guards, receivers and safeties) carry out the tasks that have been passed down from the front office to the field.

To score the game-winning touchdown, you need to run the plays the way they were laid out. Otherwise, it becomes a team of individuals, a bunch of I's operating in a world that would be better off with we's. When "The System" is not operating the way that it's supposed to, the team starts losing points or, worse still, losing altogether.

I believe that people would be more willing to be team players and less concerned with "what's in it for me," if they had to be the bull in the middle. Wait! Don't tell me you've never heard that the secret to life is to survive being the bull in the middle! Maybe I should backtrack a little. If you haven't heard about "the bull," let me be the first to lay it out for you. You take one guy – say that guy is me – place him in the center of as many of his teammates as you can rustle up, maybe 25 or 30. Make sure you accumulate plenty of those big, nasty-looking guys, who have tattoos that read, *Haven't killed anyone yet, but I will soon, and, if you're not careful, you could be the first,* give each one a number, assigned by Coach Montgomery (who I was pretty sure lay in bed at night making this stuff up). Your job is to remember at any given time who has what number and where they are relative to you, so you'll know where they'll be coming from. Because as Coach Montgomery calls out the numbers, your teammates rush at you, number by number, and knock you on your butt. Your job is to take the hit, then get up and set yourself up for the next guy to come at you.

If you keep taking it, until you're lying there in the center, down in the dirt, still trying to convince the coach to send another at you, knowing full well you're at your limit, yet prepared to do whatever it takes to get to the next level, then you aren't just a Mighty Teddy, you're a badass bull.

At first, the bull drill struck me as an exercise in insanity, but eventually I started to find it fun in the same exhilarating way that skydiving might be. Sure, it was death-defying, but it was also adrenalizing. I'd never felt more alive. Besides getting the crap kicked out of me, the "bull in the middle" game served two basic purposes: The first was to build self-confidence. The second was to see if you were paying attention, so you could anticipate whatever was coming at you. It helped us develop tenacity – not to mention catlike reflexes and memories like elephants.

So often, people talk about getting to the next level in life as if progress could be achieved through philosophical musings and wishful thinking when, in reality, progress is all about action and reaction. In retrospect, I'm not sure whether the bull in the middle drill made me better at football, but I can say for certain that it gave me the confidence to go through life prepared for the next guy who was coming to knock me on my butt.

After I did my time in the middle, another player was called to the center of the circle.

Although I gave as good as I got, my performance was nothing compared to Marshall Parks'. Marshall Parks wasn't just another athlete. He came from a family of people so naturally talented that the rest of us mere mortals could only wish we'd been so genetically blessed. Marshall had a couple of brothers who were world-class hurdlers and a sister who was universally touted as one of the most beautiful girls at school and who had a singing voice like no other. When called to the center of the ring, his presence commanded the full attention of every one of us and struck fear into our hearts, even though he was the one who should've been afraid, considering the drill was designed as a 30-against-one onslaught.

Marshall planted his feet firmly on the earth, pounding the ground beneath him with his cleats, chopping away at the earth. Coach Montgomery began calling out the numbers, each charging at our terrifying teammate one by one. Marshall answered each attack with a thunderous blow of his own, knocking down any who attempted to blindside him. Coach Montgomery picked up the pace, calling the numbers more rapidly. Marshall's feet moved faster, his cat-like reflexes placing him in the right position at the right time. He was prepared for whatever was sent his way.

Coach called my number. I charged full speed ahead, both eyes open. I hit Marshall with my best shot. He took it, gave me his, then turned to face whomever was next.

To say I was impressed is an understatement. I wanted to become as much of a master at the bull in the middle drill as the inside linebacker, so I watched and I learned, studying him so that I could become adept at expecting the unexpected. That's another thing football taught me. We can learn by observation as well as by experience.

Being part of a team, teaches you a lot about yourself and other people. There's an expression I like a lot: "I win, you win, we win and if we fall short then we lose as a team." Teams function like

THE INDISPENSABLE GAME OF X'S AND O'S

tight-knit families, and with that level of togetherness comes progress. When you can get people to work as one unit for the same goal, then it equals success, or equals success in progress. My plan wasn't ever to be a super star. I just wanted to be one of the guys. But, in order to be one of them, I needed to be prepared for everything they threw at me. I needed to be prepared to get hit.

"Get fired up!" yelled Coach Montgomery. Then, he sent me back to the center of the ring where, once again, I was to be the bull. This time, I was prepared.

Go ahead, I thought. *Try coming at me from anywhere. I'm ready. This time, I'll see it coming.*

CHAPTER 15

A PREREQUISITE TO LIVING A GOOD LIFE, IS TO HAVE FUN IN THE LIFE YOU'RE LIVING – "GET A FIGHT SONG"

My first fight song was my high school football team's fight song. We would sing it each week during the school day, and on our way to and from games, whether we were playing home or away.

The whole student body embraced our fight song:

We are the Teddies
Mighty mighty Teddies
Everywhere we go
People want to know
Who we are
So, we tell them
We are the Teddies…

We would repeat the verses over and over again.

Now that I'm a grown man with obligations and responsibilities, I still have a fight song. It's changed. The Mighty Teddies anthem has been superseded by Seal's and R-Kelly "Space Jam" original, "I Believe I Can Fly." That little ditty never fails to cast my worries aside and help me set the tone for another great day.

My days these days aren't much different than they were in high school. I'm still up early, still living my dream, and still getting inspired by a personal anthem. I consistently put in a lot of time and hard work, double my efforts and triple my sacrifices, and over and over, I find that I don't just get to stay in the starting lineup, I get promoted.

Having my own personal fight song has unlocked in me an endless capacity for getting pumped up, regardless of the circumstances. It's something I learned from my time as a Mighty

Fighting Teddy. I encourage you to adopt a fight song of your own – something you can sing every day, because it feels good deep down in your soul. I always begin my day with "I Believe I Can Fly" because when you look at my physical stature and how I was raised I shouldn't have achieved any of what I've achieved, but by taking control over what I could, I've soared.

In 1999, I was at the Lucerne Health Club on East 79th Street, where I worked as an independent personal trainer. Two of my friends, Mitch and Eric, entered the club. Both were screaming and jumping up and down as if they were doing some kind of ancient tribal dance. They circled one another, leaping into the air and screaming with ever-growing intensity, completely unaware of anyone else's presence. After watching the two of them celebrating in the middle of the room, I couldn't help but get caught up in the moment. Their fun was so contagious that I found myself hopping and hollering with them.

It was only after the celebration died down that I got them to tell me what all the rejoicing was about.

The two of them had hit a home run in the stock market, at least that's how Mitch described it. Although I didn't know exactly what a home run meant in terms of actual dollar-and-cent financial gains, I understood that it was a win. A big win. Their public display was the Wall Street version of a fight song, with some dancing thrown in for effect.

"This is what it's all about," Mitch said to Eric. "We may have missed a few every now and then, but today we guessed right."

Eric, singing the high note, replied, "This is like good sex."

They jumped up some more, exchanged a couple of congratulatory high fives, and exited the gym without ever working out.

I know first-hand how difficult it can be not to give up when you keep getting knocked on your butt. I took my first big hit back when I was in the third grade, abandoned by my mother and dropped off at my grandparents'. But I didn't cry "Woe is me!" and stay there, sobbing on the ground. Okay, I may have wallowed a little, but I soon found football, structure, friendship, and a fight song.

There's no better feeling than doing what others say can't be done. No more satisfying achievement than realizing your dreams despite all the obstacles to achieving them. Home runs are always sweeter after strikeouts. Maybe, I should jump up and do a little dance in the middle of the room now, because if anyone is reading this book or listening to it on audio tape, then my words on these pages are proof that if you keep getting up after life has knocked you down, that everything is possible. If you can see it, it can be done. Believe you can fly.

CHAPTER 16

‗‗‗

THE INDISPENSABLE GAME OF X'S AND O'S

In football, every team has a playbook. Coach Clemens referred to our playbook as "The map to our success." As a freshman player, new to the game, I studied ours, memorizing the X's and O's to learn not only what I was supposed to do but the movements of my teammates and every possible scenario for how our opponents might react.

I've come to believe that every one of us ought to create our own playbook. In fact, journal-keeping has served this exact purpose in my life. Not only do I record memorable moments that have already happened. I plan and strategize for what lies ahead, foreseeing possibilities and knowing the movements I intend to make well before I make them. And I read. I consider reading an essential part of my developmental process and firmly believe it ought to be emphasized in our culture as one of the pillars of success. I might not have caught up with Pops, but I read a lot.

Looking back, Pops' example served a pivotal role in keeping me from succumbing to stereotypes. As a young black kid who once fled from the Chains of Rap Brown, I could've easily grown up to become one of society's many I-don't-read-for-pleasure-ers. Instead, I've developed an unparalleled love of learning. It's a tragedy to me that there are many in this country who don't value literature. On the West Coast, they put on the books a new language called "Ebonics." As far as I'm concerned, Ebonics isn't a reclamation of language, a subversive form of power, or a symbol of nonconformity. It's English for those too lazy to learn to read and speak properly. It's a forced fit. A square peg trying to fit into a round hole.

I'm not knocking anyone that has mastered the language, but Ebonics doesn't fit into "The System" of Harvard, Ohio State, UCLA, Penn State, IBM, Microsoft, Wall Street, and other such institutions of greatness. It won't take those who study it to the next level of higher learning, or higher living. I was once the personal trainer to a rapper who told me, "If you want to keep something secret, put it in a book."

It saddened me to think that literature, a phenomenal resource for expansion and empowerment, could be so grossly overlooked. I knew two things: he was right, and he didn't have to be.

One day, when Uncle Bill and I were walking in the park, he explained that a child's failure and success started with his parents. "Failure and success are learned behaviors," he told me. "Any parent who questions the actions of their child should first look at themselves, hence the phrase 'The apple doesn't fall far from the tree.'" Although what he said that day made and still makes a lot of sense to me, I've come to believe that his perspective is too simplistic.

There are some rare cases where, even the most vibrant tree yields "bad seeds," and others where the most unfruitful of trees yields rare and wonderful fruit. For the most part though, Uncle Bill's observations were accurate. Life begins in childhood and if parents don't have a plan and purpose for raising their offspring, the results will be evident.

Imagine that you're building a brand-new house. When you first set out, you dreamed of having a great room for entertaining. You wanted imported marble tile, 24-karat gold leaf trim on the walls and priceless artwork on the walls, but to have this room, your dream room, you realize that you're over budget. To have the great room of your dreams, you'll need to cut back on expenses somewhere else, so you decide to skimp on the foundation. Nobody will ever see the foundation anyway.

Fast forward. You've got a brand-new home, the American dream, a place to raise your family for the next 35-40 years. You've even got your dream great room. You're so happy with the house you've built that you forget it's built on a weak foundation. What do you think will happen at the first sign of a rainstorm?

It's no surprise that many people end up flooded or crumbling in the face of the slightest adversity. On the other hand, if we focus on erecting solid, well-made foundations, whatever we build will stand the test of time.

For those of us who have, or are planning to have, children, it's essential to understand that, from the moment our offspring takes his or her first breath, he or she is taking in information. Protect and love your children unconditionally, allowing their little bodies and minds to grow. Begin reading to them as early and as often as possible, opening their precious minds to all the wonders of the world.

May I suggest, *Sprinkles, The True Spirit of Christmas* is a great book to start with. Don't wait for the movie to come out (the movies are never as good as the book), *Sprinkles, The True Spirit of Christmas* is the foundation for a film to come.

Unlike any other mammal, human babies depend solely on their parents for survival. And, yet, a lot of parents fail their children from the start. They neglect to stimulate their children's minds or to equip them for success by feeding them properly or encouraging physical activity. This becomes a setup for a life that's lacking in personal fulfillment. In fact, there have been many documented studies that conclusively demonstrate that reading to a child is crucial. Especially in the early stages. Between the ages of zero and one, a child can take in and retain information three times more quickly than a child 15 to 18. I've observed this firsthand in my own children. They never cared about the content of whatever I was reading. All they cared about was the soothing sound of my voice as I communicated sentiments that went beyond words.

Not only does reading to children teach them whatever lessons are contained in a book. It offers a powerful message that you love them enough to spend time with them. It assures them that they can count on you to keep repeating and relaying X's and O's until they learn "The System" well enough to decipher its playbook without you.

I was seldom read to as a child. Even when she was still around, my mother wasn't very present as a parent and my father was too preoccupied with himself to carve out time for story-time. Pops was fond of sharing isolated passages or relating quotes, but I can't recall a regular reading ritual until I had children of my own. This may have contributed to my childhood reluctance to read. During my early life, I was ashamed to read out loud. I wasn't exactly the best reader.

Although no one talked about ADHD when I was growing up, I later learned that the fact that when I looked at the words on a page, they shifted was a symptom of something other than youthful inattention. Even today, whenever I read out loud, I feel a pang of apprehension. But I don't let it stop me. I love the written word and have come to see reading as a life practice.

Throughout our children's early years, while my ex-wife and I were parenting together, and after we began co-parenting apart, between the two of us, we never missed a single day of reading to our children. My ex was an avid reader, far more adept than I. But we were both completely committed to the sanctity of story time.

Turns out, our kids didn't care if I stumbled over a couple of words every now and then. The only thing that mattered was the love and affection that reading to them conveyed.

Don't get me wrong. I'm not saying that a child that is not read to by their parents will never become highly motivated or successful, but developing minds are especially susceptible to the stimulus of learning and reading to our children provides them with a competitive and early edge. The sooner you can stimulate young brain cells, the better.

The written word is just like the playbook I had from my football days. Each book I am blessed to open proceeds to open my mind. It shows me powerful possibilities that I never would've had access to without being exposed to the words and wisdom it contains.

Whenever I'm at a bookstore or a library or perusing Amazon's online paper book and hardcover offerings, I think about Pops and smile. If you take nothing more from this book, please remember this: Not reading robs our minds, justifies our fears, and slowly eviscerates our souls, whereas reading expands our minds' capacity, infusing them with new ideas and enabling us to arrive at previously unseen possibilities.

CHAPTER 17

NO APOLOGIES NEEDED

Larry Hightower, "Buddy" as we called him, was the best fullback in the Dayton High School system of schools. His on-field prowess was talked about not only at Roosevelt High but throughout much of Ohio. Herb Smith, Big Tank, Larry Lee, Jason Kirkland, Jason Thompson, the Powell twins, and the Kelly brothers were the best at their positions, too. Our varsity squad was the team to beat, even though others seldom beat us. When people in the city of Dayton talked about competition, they talked of the Mighty Teddies. To be on the team was an honor and a privilege. I was part of a winning system with a rich history.

Coach Montgomery always emphasized that, even at the top – especially at the top – there was no such thing as coasting. "Get used to big competition, because although you don't know it now, you will be competing big for the rest of your life!"

Contrary to what many people assume, at the highest levels, success is mostly mental. We worked hard, sure. (I've told you all about the wind sprints and the bull in the middle drill). But what's really required to become and stay a winner are mental agility, adaptability, preparation, and the willingness to give everything you've got, holding nothing back, not day by day, but minute by minute, second by second.

There are some who might say that winning shouldn't be the bottom line, that what really matters is how you play the game. I'm not buying. If winning didn't matter, why would anyone sacrifice his or her time away from home and family to be on the fast track of moving up that corporate ladder? What purpose would be playing the market serve if not to put you in a better financial position? What good would it do to be the best in your class if you couldn't be picked first for the best jobs? Just playing the game isn't enough. The goal in life is to get to the next level. And, in order to do that, a person needs to develop a way to quantify their performance and adjust accordingly. Self-evaluation is critical. Developing a winning strategy and measuring success or failure based on results is the surest way to get from where you currently are to where you want to be.

Sometimes, it seems that our culture expects people to apologize for their triumphs and gladly accept defeat. This is senseless. Do you think Flow Jo, Michael Jordan, LeBron James, Serena Williams, Venus Williams, Billy Jean King, Usain Bolt, Chrissy Wellington, or Steph Curry ever said they were sorry for their victories? Steph Curry has a championship ring for each of his fingers, whereas Charles and Patrick have none. But the Golden Boy of the Golden State has never asked forgiveness after scoring 60 points, when he could have scored 30 and still won the game. Life operates on a Play to Win system. That's the bottom line. No one should ever be made to feel bad about themselves for having winning as their goal.

In the late 1990s, when I was still working as a personal trainer in New York City, one of my clients David Hammoto, who my then-wife and I had become friends with, invited us to spend a weekend at their South Hampton house.

On the way there, my wife began to lecture me. "Don't be the way you always are, Kevin."

"What do you mean?"

"I want a restful weekend, not for you and David to spend the whole weekend trying to one-up each other."

Most of my friends, or should I say all my friends, and I love to compete. We compete against ourselves and we compete against each other. We challenge one another to be better. My wife didn't understand this way of relating to anyone, especially David, who was both a friend and a client. She asked me to be a good houseguest by letting David win. I didn't understand. David wasn't the kind of guy who needed any help beating me, or anyone else. He came from a ridiculously endowed trust fund and had been given a golf course in Honolulu, Hawaii as a birthday gift from a family friend who didn't have kids and loved him like a son. He went to one of the best schools in the country, landed a job with one of the largest financial groups in the world, had a beautiful home on Fifth Avenue, a great wife, and two perfect kids. To top it off, he was an all-around good guy and a phenomenal friend. But my wife maintained that beating a person you do business with in his own home could spoil our business and personal relationships.

The idea that my competitive nature would do harm to my relationships struck me as ridiculous. I was taught that giving anything other than your absolute best ought to be classified a sin. But I also learned from being out in the real world that, for it to count, winning has to be done within "The System." for it to count. Playing the game without knowing all the rules can be the equivalent of picking up a fumbled football and running full speed ahead only to realize that you've run toward the wrong end zone and scored a touchdown on yourself.

Maybe what my wife was saying had some merit. I thought about it. Would it be a win to do my best or to hold back?

I'd conditioned myself to play all-out in every area of life. So, what if it was just a weekend in South Hampton, New York (the playground of the wealthy)? It was also a microcosm of the macrocosm. We were two men at the peak of our games. David came into this world with one foot placed in the doorway of success. I came from a place most would like to forget, but which I have chosen to remember.

Round ball (basketball) was David's chosen sport. I was at somewhat of a disadvantage. Basketball was the only organized team sport I had ever been cut from. Plus, both knees had blown out within 18 months of one another. But I could still get all five of my fingers above the rim, and with whatever God-given speed I'd managed to retain, I was still faster than most. David and I played. He pushed. I pushed back. He scored. I scored. I had made my decision the moment I stepped onto the court. I'd play the game the way I lived my life, with attitude, passion, and purpose.

We played the best out of five. He took the first game, me the next three. We went out for a road race. He beat me by a couple of steps. We moved on to wind sprints. At the end of it all, we were closer – and more competitive – than ever. We might've been playing to win, yet we saw ourselves as a team, each of us contributing to the other by pushing him to be better. We knew the fundamental truth: In life, the most decisive game you'll ever play is the one within yourself.

CHAPTER 18

THE CRYING GAME

Looking at myself in the mirror, I saw a different person than the one who'd first run onto the football field with my dad watching proudly, and unsuspectingly, from above. That didn't mean I'd arrived. Sure, I'd made it to mid-season and been promoted to the "suicide squad," but I wanted more.

My time was divided between playing and practicing with my freshman teammates and with the varsity suicide. Week after week, I found myself cleaning the dirt from the practice field from my facemask and jersey. Each time I stood on the sidelines and watched the bigger, faster, meaner guys board the bus, dressed in the most amazing red and white jerseys with two thin blue stripes on each sleeve, and their helmets bearing the design of the Mighty Teddy bear – whose fangs and claws almost jumped off the sides of the helmet – I'd feel the same stirrings of resolve I had the day I went into Coach Russo's office and asked him what I had to do to earn a spot on the varsity squad.

During football season, Fridays were a big day at school. The varsity players could wear their game jerseys. They would parade around the hallways on their way to and from class looking and acting like they owned the place, which they did.

Each varsity player was afforded an almost God-like status. Students and teachers alike would be swept up in anticipation of that night's game. Well-wishers and wannabes bumped the varsity guys' chests and slapped them with the highest of high fives. Moments after the last bell dismissed us for the day, anyone with a car and anyone hoping to bum a ride to the game rushed out to the parking lot to adorn their rides with as much red and white as they could lay their hands on. It was the high school equivalent of a tailgate party, on a much lower scale and budget. As for me, I ran over to Grace A. Green practice field with the rest of my freshman teammates where, as part of the rich tradition of the Mighty Teddies, we watched our idols board the bus.

As I stood admiring the bus-bound players from afar, I felt my chest swell. Suddenly alone in a crowd of many, I began to sing the Mighty Teddy fight song louder than everyone around me.

"I'm a Mighty Teddy!" I belted out. Even though I remained a lowly freshman and an oft-flattened member of the suicide squad, I felt a bond with the big guys that permeated deep down into me.

"Hurry!" I enthused as I sat in the backseat of an upperclassman's car.

After the bus pulled out of the parking lot, I'd bummed a ride over to the stadium. On varsity game days, in lieu of practice, we freshmen were expected to sit in the stands and show our support.

My mind turned everything into a competition. I wanted to beat the team bus. We didn't. By the time we arrived at the stadium, both sets of varsity players were warming up. On one side of the stadium, the Roosevelt High supporters were singing the fight song of the Mighty Teddies, 1500 strong. On the other side was Dayton Roth singing their fight song.

In the 1970s in Dayton, each of the high schools had practice fields, but there was only one game field. Each school, whether designated home or away, showed up on game day to play all out for stands full of fans. Our side seemed to be louder, but I'm sure if someone had polled the other side, they'd have claimed the same about their volume.

I figured it didn't matter. We were the better team. Our school had an impressive history of having the best of the best in all our sports programs, both men's and women's. In the house of the Mighty Teddies, winning was contagious. In fact, up until this night, our season's win/loss record was perfect.

The Roosevelt and Dayton Roth captains met in the center of the field. The uniformed official flicked a small silver disk into the air. The coin fell to the turf. Dayton Roth won the toss and elected to kick off. We took the southeast side of the field to defend. I took my seat in the ice-cold stands with the other 1499 fans who had come out on a cold fall night to cheer for the Mighty Teddies. We cheered loudly on every play, both good and bad, and by halftime, when the teams retired to their respective locker rooms, the score was even at six points apiece. I found myself boasting to all the surrounding spectators that I was more than just a freshman footballer. I was a member of the suicide squad, which meant I'd played a role – however small – in the varsity team's ongoing greatness. Or that's what I told myself (and anyone who would listen).

We heard the Mighty Teddies return before we saw them. The sound of the familiar fight song and a stampede of feet… If possible, they were even more determined than before. It was as if the battle had never stopped.

The second half was not much different than the first. Dayton Roth pushed us to one end of the field. We pushed them to the other. The team we thought we'd beat was proving a formidable opponent. The intensity and determination were so thick you could cut them with a knife. I couldn't sit still. I wanted to do my part. I wanted to play. I wanted the ball. Instead, I held tight to my hot dog, ketchup running over the side of my hand, and watched ineffectually. The score remained tied at 6 to 6. The fourth quarter rolled around. With nearly nothing left on the clock, Roth elected to kick a 48-yard field goal, an almost impossible feat in high school football.

On the sidelines, our coaches huddled together to solidify an overtime strategy. They were as certain as all of us in the stands that the kicker would miss.

Roth's kicker lined himself up with the ball. The whistle blew. The clock continued ticking down. The opposing player approached the ball with determination. My eyes looked toward the goal post, waiting for the pigskin missile to hit or miss its intended target. But there was no thud. No 48-yard field goal kick. They faked it. The holder took off with the ball and tossed it to a wide-open end, who caught it and ran it into the end zone. They won. It was our first loss of the season, to a team that, according to the stats, we should have beaten.

I hurried over to the bus to lend my support to my fallen warrior brothers. My intentions were to tell them it had been a hard-fought game and we'd "get-'em next time," but when I got there my words caught in my throat. The mightiest of the mighty, the big tough guys, the best in the city of Dayton, the all-city, all-state athletes, were boarding the bus with their heads hung low. Some were mad. Others had tears in their eyes.

I'd never seen a grown man cry before. In my house, men weren't allowed to cry. My dad said a man crying was a sign of weakness, and that, if a man had done his best, there was no need to shed a tear. But these were the Mighty Teddies. I'd witnessed them battle valiantly. There was nothing they should be holding their heads down about.

I approached Larry Hightower, the team's star running back. Larry had taken a liking to me. During practice, every time he ran me over, he would always be there with a smirk, a helping hand and an "at-a-boy."

I figured the man who had just rushed for just over 100 yards and scored the team's only rushing touchdown and had just talked to the reporters who stopped him, would want to talk to his little buddy. He didn't. When he saw me coming, Larry Hightower turned away. I wasn't sure why. No one who'd witnessed his, or any other Mighty Teddy's performance could have said anything bad about the way they played. They were in the game from start to finish. It was just that the other team got a lucky break and scored a touchdown when there wasn't any more time on the clock.

But people like Larry Hightower are different than the me I used to be. When you're all-city three years in a row, all-state twice, and have been the starting running back for the Mighty Teddies from freshman until senior year, the tear that runs from the corner of your eye, down the side of your face, and hangs like a tightrope walker, waiting to be saved by your shirt sleeve, isn't an emotional expression of your innermost feelings. It's a yardstick, measuring your successes and your failures.

People like Larry love winning, yes, but, more than anything, they hate losing. As Larry boarded the bus, it began to rain. I stood staring after the bus full of the best football players I'd ever met. There would be no fight song on the ride back to the Roosevelt High parking lot, just sadness and silence. That was the moment I internalized a lesson I still carry with me to this day. One can't simply measure himself according to desire. Outcomes are important. A man's successes and failures matter. Life is a game and every time you come up short, you must own the loss.

A lot of people will tell you that winning isn't everything, that it's how you play the game that matters. If that's true, then why bother to keep score?

Anyone who's ever been at the top will tell you that being there is in and of itself a powerful experience. Lucky for me, I learned the values of hard work, preparation, short and long-term goal setting, and perseverance early on. Pops, Uncle Bill, and even Dad made it clear that success was earned and that excuses were irrelevant. What they'd neglected to impart, either by their words or their example, was that when the stakes were high, a man could suffer heartbreak.

Larry Hightower was the first man I ever saw cry and I'm grateful that was the case. Because of who I knew Larry to be, and how much he meant to me, I didn't think any less of him for caring so much about winning that it hurt him to lose.

It would be years later before I realized that sadness isn't the only reason for tears. The great Bo Jackson cried the day he received his college degree, a promise he'd made to his mother after he turned pro. She died a year before he was to walk across the stage. Michael Jordan cried after winning his fifth NBA championship for his dad. I cried for the first time, openly and without reservation, as I held my hands out to catch my son, Theo, when he fell out of the birth canal and into the world. Delivering my own son was one of the greatest and most emotional moments of my life. Despite the misconception about manliness being unemotional, the men I looked up to felt deeply. Yet, their feelings were inextricably linked to their sense of purpose. That said, I don't advocate gratuitous emotional outpourings or self-indulgent pity-parties, but rather the high-stakes, fully-invested attitude that I learned watching my high school heroes board the bus, screaming and shouting, on the way to the game and return to that same bus, heads down and silent, for the return ride back to school.

The tear that dangled from the side of Larry Hightower face wasn't there because he was feeling sorry for himself. It was there because he hated losing more than he loved winning. And he recognized that the team hadn't had to lose. It wasn't inevitable. Like the rest of the Mighty Teddies, his heart was heavy with the weight of lost opportunity. Each was evaluating himself and his performance, assessing how he'd failed and coming up with a strategy for outperforming himself when he next had the chance. Watching the young men who had become my living, breathing gods, I understood that effort would never be enough. For a winner, effort mattered, yes, but what was even more important were outcomes.

As I headed back toward the car that would take me home, my own head low in solidarity, I arrived at a critical distinction that has remained with me ever since.

There are two kinds of people: Those who truly want success, and those who are simply trying to avoid failure. I vowed to always strive for success. I was determined to be a Mighty Teddy.

CHAPTER 19

TIP DRILLS

The Monday after the big loss, as soon as school let out, I hustled over to the practice field. Anticipating that the varsity players would still be in bad moods, I wanted to get my gear on and be out of the locker room before they arrived. But, by the time I got there, they were already there. Not only that. To my surprise, they were jocular, acting as if Friday's game had never happened.

Larry Hightower's tears were gone. He was smiling broadly, joking with the other guys and behaving as if he hadn't ever felt the pang of disappointment.

I stood, stymied, in front of my locker until a loud voice boomed out from the opposite side of the room. "Hey McLemore!"

I spun around. "Yes, Coach Montgomery?"

The coach beckoned me into his office. I followed, hoping I hadn't inadvertently done anything wrong.

Coach wasn't angry. Far from it. He told me that he wanted me to begin practicing with the varsity squad, then he threw a red varsity practice jersey into my face, with the number 67 printed on it. I wasn't the only one from the freshman team who got one of those nice new practice jerseys that day. Jason, Marshall, Big Al, and a couple other guys got theirs, too. Larry Lee was already on the Varsity team, the only freshman to start varsity and go pro. He played for the Detroit Lions.

I donned my new practice jersey, then hustled down to the field. I hadn't caught on yet that all my hard work had paid off, and that I had gotten to where I said I wanted to be in the time frame I'd said I wanted to get there.

Larry Hightower led the team's practice warmups. Each time he barked an impassioned order, the vein in the middle of his head seemed as if it was going to burst.

"Hit the ground!" he yelled.

We dropped!

"Up!" he yelled.

We jumped to our feet. "Now chop those feet! Faster!"

The ground shook as we pounded the earth. "Down on the ground, 100 pushups, sets of twenty. He said it, we did it.

"Who are we!" he yelled.

"The Mighty Teddies!" we responded.

"I can't hear you!"

The 44 of us were face down in the dirt yet eager for more.

He yelled again. "Who are we!"

With even more power, we roared our response. Our voices echoed through the area, booming through the nearby projects and reverberating until we were surrounded by the sound of ourselves.

"We are the Mighty Teddies!" We hit the ground again, then roared, up and down, and up again.

Larry was a miniature coach in the making, one of us and yet somehow so much more. As our team captain, destined for success, he inspired by example. He shouted louder, hustled harder, and cared more than anyone and we knew that it was because he loved us that he always demanded our best. As warm-ups were coming to an end, as if Moses had returned, Coach Montgomery's voice parted the sea of sounds. He ordered us to assemble in the center of the field. I took my new gear and headed toward the front row, but the big guys – now my teammates – pushed me out of their way. I retreated to the back where all the new guys were supposed to stand.

There was a very long pause during which Coach took the time to lock eyes with every young man out there, as if he could peer into the essence of us, which I'd come to believe he could. Then, as soft as a lion's gentle whisper just before a roar, Coach Montgomery spoke. He talked about the performance of the team during the previous Friday's performance.

He told us that he'd done the math and figured out we had knocked down or batted away so many passes, that, if we'd caught at least two of them, we could have scored the one or two extra touchdowns or field goals needed to ensure victory, and never have ended up in the situation we did – the situation that cost us the game.

"They didn't beat us," he said. "We beat ourselves. When we win, we win as a team, and when we lose, we're still that same team. So, we're going back to basics. We're going to work on tip drills. We're going to do them until you'd rather be dead than let another ball pass through your hands."

Tip drills were new to me. I'd gotten good at running and at being knocked around. I'd even acquired a reputation for having total disregard for my own body. But the nuances were something I'd never appreciated before.

Coach called us over to the sideline, separated us into clusters, then instructed each group to stand in front of the other coaches. Each group was assigned a coach and each coach held a football in his hands.

"Those who drop run wind sprints until I get tired of watching you!" Coach Montgomery yelled.

I went to the back of the line so I could watch and learn before my turn came. Coach tossed the ball to one guy, who tipped it into the air, and the next guy behind him tried to catch the ball before it hits the ground.

Nothing to it, I thought.

After observing a couple of guys go through the tip drill thing, I convinced myself that it was pretty simple. And, it turned out, tip drills were for me. I had excellent hands. All I needed was to watch and learn so I'd know what the hell I was supposed to do.

I didn't realize it during the drill, but, after practice, Coach Russo pulled me aside and informed me that tip drills were about two things: poise and concentration.

In a controlled environment like practice, it was easy to walk the fine tightrope between composure and focus, but in game situations it became much harder to execute. Practicing situations where we'd need to snatch errant balls out of the air (quite literally) drilled the skillset into us in the hopes that we'd become so adept at catching them that, even during game-time, pressure-cooker situations, it would be second nature.

Composure is essential, both in life and in athletics. I'm glad I learned that lesson early and had it reinforced often. There are many stellar athletes whose lack of it has caused them and others a lot of unnecessary suffering and for whom bad behavior during and outside of game-time has actively sabotaged their success. One such example is Dennis Rodman. In his prime, Rodman was the best defensive player in the NBA. Many would argue that point, but the record books don't lie. He was the best rebounder in the NBA. I was never bothered by what color his hair happened to be, nor was I inspired by the messages he'd had scrawled upon his body, or the gender-bending clothing he proudly chose to wear. On the court, Dennis was the best of the best. But far too often, he lost his composure, and, because of that, he and his teammates suffered.

The moment Rodman stepped out on that hardwood; the referees were watching him closer than any other player on the floor. Every eye was on him. What other players could get away with, he couldn't. Because Dennis couldn't get out of his own way, his natural skills and talent would inevitably fall by the wayside. At any given moment, an opposing player, a ref, or even one of his own teammates, could throw him off his game.

Luckily for him, Rodman was in the right places with the right people at the right time, which is the reason he owns so many championships rings, yet when most people think about the legacy he left behind, they think about multiple fines, suspensions and lawsuits. Even after he retired from the game, scandals continued to follow him. Or, more accurately, he continued to create scandals because he couldn't exhibit self-restraint.

Anyone who has skyrocketed to success while simultaneously commanding widespread admiration possesses poise and concentration. Oprah, Bo Jackson, Michael Jordan, Julius Erving, Penny Marshall, Walter Payton, and Ellen DeGeneres, among others, are more than merely talented. They're self-possessed even in the face of challenging situations. In 1998, when the beef industry sued Oprah, she remained a pillar of decorum and emerged victorious. Perhaps Rodman would've done well to learn from her example considering that, in the same year, he missed a mandatory media appearance and was fined $10,000.

As a fitness professional for more than 35 years, I have been fortunate enough to work with hundreds of men and women. This has enabled me to acquire the skillset to distinguish between those that are merely good and those that are destined for greatness. If you look into the eyes of any world-class athlete, you can practically see their brains working like high speed computers with super powered hard drives. They have so much information stored within their memories that their minds operate like the most modern MACs, whereas the rest of us are the equivalent of 1980s PCs.

Tip drills were a powerful reminder of the need to remain anchored in the present moment while moving toward a winning future. Coach Montgomery had us do them until it was as if we'd been outfitted with blinders. Not blinders in any pejorative sense of the word, but the sort of powerful focusing agents designed to stop us from looking at anything other than what mattered, to let go of looking back at things over which we had no control, to stop projecting into the future, and to concentrate on what was important – catching the ball.

"Keep your eyes on the ball," Coach Montgomery yelled out to us, over and over again, "and the ball out of the sky!"

My suppositions about the value of remaining concentrated, purposeful, and poised don't just apply to sports heroes, or even everyday athletes. This every word in this book is directed toward the average person who wants to be more than just average. Consider this: What if you spent most of your time concentrating on one thing, doing it repeatedly until you got it right? Wouldn't that have positive and powerful implications in your life? Unwavering concentration makes you oblivious to life's distractions and enables you to perform at your peak potential. That will catapult you out of average and into extraordinary. If we could all learn to select a goal, then stay fixed and focused on the purpose at hand, more people would realize their dreams.

They say that words inspire heroic deeds, but it is well-known that actions have an even greater impact than words.

There is truth to the saying, "Nothing ventured; nothing gained." Several years back, during the final game of the NBA championship, I witnessed a moment that will be forever burned in my heart and mind. The news reports that day said that Michael Jordan had the flu. It was questionable whether he could even compete. But when the lights came up and the players hit the floor, Michael hustled out onto the court along with his teammates. Weak and running a high fever, he was determined that he was going to do as much as he could to bring his city another championship. He played hard every minute out on the court, and when he was brought to the bench to get much-needed fluids into his system, he lay on the floor with the cameras fixed on him, resting briefly and shaking with sickness. Then, as soon as each timeout was over, he jumped to his feet and took to the floor.

Even though many of his more compassionate friends and fans had repeatedly urged him to step down and let his team play while he recuperated, Jordan was a man on a mission. He ran up and down the court with as much outward energy as a rookie playing his very first game. Everyone watching Jordan's performance questioned how long he would be able to keep up his breakneck pace while staving off the flu, but he didn't so much as falter. He kept his poise and concentration.

Every shot he took was fixed on the bigger picture. As the clock ran down, even though he must've felt dead on his feet, he moved to the left, then the right, then he pulled up and took the last shot. When it was all said and done, and the game was over, his team triumphant, Jordan fell into the arms of teammate and friend, Scotty Pippin.

Jordan's performance is an example of what becomes possible when we live our lives with passion, focus, and preparation. Stay focused, have a vision that can't be redirected, be open to improving yourself and acquiring the necessary skills, learn from every loss and never settle for anything less than your best. This is as true for a world-renowned athlete, a six-year-old competing against eight and ten-year-olds, and regular folks, like you and me.

Coach Montgomery oversaw and implemented our reconditioning via tip drills, he was imbedding a powerful lesson into us. Sure, others saw us as the best of the best, but that wasn't enough. We were capable of more than we'd displayed. He was teaching us never to be comfortable with just being good. Good wasn't good enough. We needed to be great.

Mastering your craft and making sure you're ready every time the ball comes your way doesn't just lift you up, it elevates your entire team. There is greatness in all of us, however, there are only a select few that choose to be great. By being upbeat, living positively, working hard, and never allowing yourself to be waylaid by a flu, a disqualification due to age, or any other circumstance or consideration, you can score the winning shot. You can be unstoppable and unforgettable. You can make an impact. You can break the tape.

CHAPTER 20

FUNDAMENTALLY SOUND

The past determines the future. That doesn't mean every action we ever take will have future ramifications, or that it's not possible to course-correct at any time. But there's no denying that where we are today is a direct result of our aggregate yesterdays.

As I stand here, at the age of sixty, taking stock of my situation, I can clearly see how my ability to navigate "The System" has determined my level of success. No matter who you are or where you are in life, if you apply and adapt "The System" to almost any problem, short of death or dying, it becomes inevitable that you will achieve a solution.

No matter how gifted or talented you are, no matter what your profession, you can't escape the fundamentals of the game of life. Two people who, on paper, are equally skilled in their trade can, and often do, end up on opposite sides of the success spectrum. Why? Because, if one of them is willing to work hard, set goals, learn from their mistakes, and push themselves, they will soar, whereas regardless of potential the other is likely to sink.

I once sat in on a conversation where a young man who had worked for one of the biggest accounting firms in New York City was telling a story about how he had been "unappreciated" and "overlooked." According to this man, he and two women had been members of the same graduating class. On paper, they were no different from one another. All three had master's degrees and all three were employed by the same company at the same starting job and with similar salaries. Upon their hiring by the firm, and over the years, each of the employees had been told they were on the "partner track," meaning that, based on performance, they stood to receive a big promotion, an ownership interest in the business, and greater financial rewards.

Over the years it took for these three individuals to make their way from associates to managers and then to be put up for partner consideration, changes occurred in each of their lives. One of the women had become a mother, and between balancing work and family, she had initially approached the firm's managing partners to tell them she wasn't interested in remaining on the partner track and, in fact, was looking to step down. She didn't want a new role or the expanded responsibilities it required. Her superiors persuaded her to reconsider her position. This woman had proven herself an invaluable asset. A real team player, she had made a massive difference both within the company and within the community at large. She had been profiled in a couple of major magazines, which had put her corporation into the public eye as a frontrunner among women-friendly companies. In many ways, she'd solidified her status as a powerful force within the industry, yet she was more than a mere figurehead. A creative thinker, an innovative problem-solver and a dynamic and well-networked professional, she was beloved by clients and the firm knew that losing her would not only have devastating consequences to their bottom line but would negatively impact their reputation in the industry. They implored her to remain on the partner track then proceeded to lay out a win/win scenario which would not only solve her work/family imbalance situation but would bring the company into the 21st century as a female-friendly, family-forward place to work.

The company incentivized her stay by allowing her to work an 80% schedule, of which she only had to report to work physically a couple of times per week. The other days she could work from home. Then, the company set her up with every convenience she would need to keep in touch with her clients, as well as her subordinates, peers, and superiors. This was a huge undertaking for both the employee and the firm. It set an important precedent that proved a compelling incentive for new hires and gave the company a competitive edge.

Not only did the woman for whom this new program was created agree to this scenario and fulfil all the outlined expectations, she out-performed many of her co-workers who were physically at work every day, operating on full-time schedules and receiving full-time salaries. She brought in new business for the firm, even saving a few precarious accounts. Never mind that she was working from the comfort of her home, her two kids screaming and crying in the background, she was a captain of industry, excelling in every aspect of business and inspiring those around her to greatness.

The other woman in this hired-together, partnership-track threesome performed her job equally well. While working 60-hour work weeks, she simultaneously attended night school to continue to further her education and get a second master's, a qualification that made her more marketable and increased her reputation both inside and outside of the firm. Meanwhile, despite her busy schedule, she maintained good relationships with her clients and co-workers, adding value whenever opportunities arose. And she never took a single day off from either work or school.

The male hiree, on the other hand, did only what was expected of him. Sure, he logged a lot of overtime, serviced his clients, hit his numbers, and even played a couple rounds of golf with one of the senior partners. But he lacked initiative and didn't make himself indispensable.

When the time came for the company to offer partner positions, when it came time for promotions, both women were offered partnerships while the firm asked the man to wait two more years until another opening became available. Even then, they told him, they couldn't guarantee a promotion. They said they valued him as an employee, yet it was clear from their unwillingness to offer him a partnership that he'd failed to make himself an essential member of the organization.

After speaking with this clearly disgruntled man and hearing his tale of imaginary woe, I understood why he'd been passed over. In the very demanding and sometimes hostile environment of the "all boys" network that exists in corporate America, these women set themselves apart. The man didn't. Based on his gender and pedigree, he had every advantage. He should've been a shoe in. Conversely, the women were a couple of Dayton Roths facing off against the Mighty Teddies. They worked harder, played smarter, and never let up. They were creative. Strategic. They took initiative. They welcomed challenges. They added so much value that the firm was willing to do whatever it took to retain them. Contrary to what the man maintained; it wasn't the women's fault he didn't make partnership. They didn't beat him. He beat himself.

Without the challenge of digging deep and playing full-out, life wouldn't be nearly as rewarding. The sooner a person realizes this, the better off they'll be. Who'd care about succeeding if success was a foregone conclusion? Scoring the winning touchdown in the final seconds of the game is only a big deal when both sides are fighting hard to win. Edging out someone who was just as good as you for that much-coveted promotion offers a rush, not in spite of all the struggling and striving, the late nights and early mornings, the meetings, and the accumulated moments of triumph, but because of them.

If we choose to go for the life we want, we are destined to embark on a series of nonstop challenges. If we spend all our limited existence backing away from obstacles and avoiding opportunities for hard-won growth, we miss out on more than we will ever know. It's a bit like getting an invitation to a party you've desperately been wanting to attend, a rare and wonderful party that you've daydreamed about with a guest list full of people you love, worship and admire, then RSVP-ing no. Or, worse yet, for those who try briefly then quit when things are no longer convenient, or require more than expected, I can liken it to getting that same invite to that same phenomenal party, showing up, having the best time of their life, then going home mid-festivities because the host is temporarily out of ice. Sometimes, a person is at the party, having a blast, knowing the night is going to keep getting steadily better and more fun, but they leave early because some inner voice tells them to run away from anything good and settle instead for boredom and mediocrity.

There's a question I've heard bandied about that I understand intellectually if not experientially. The question is "How good can you stand it?" For whatever reason, and there are a multitude of

70

them, some people flee from what's great. They fear it and they succumb to this fear. This escapism is counterproductive. The more times you run away, the better you get at it. Eventually, running away becomes a habit, and, like any other habit, the more you practice it, the more automatic it becomes. If you fail to challenge your inner self long enough, you might remain technically alive, but you'll never feel alive, and you'll never experience even a fraction of what's possible for you.

I'm confident that, if you've read this far, you're not the type to leave the party early. Even if you've left early in the past, my guess is that you've made a commitment not to do that anymore. Congratulations. Your life can only get better if you not only remain at the party but arrive early, stay until every other guest has left, offer to help out, and infuse the place with so much fun and energy that you're sure to get invited to every subsequent party, too.

No one can reach their full potential unless they consistently step out of their comfort zone. Regularly, repeatedly, answer life's invitations. Doggedly pursue your dreams. Never allow yourself to allow fear to derail you from reaching for what you want. Fear is only part of your imagination; success is on the other side of fear. Dreams come true only for those who act upon them.

If you're worried about failing, I'm here to tell you that you're going to fail. It's inevitable. You will experience moments of loss, hurt, heartbreak, disappointment, even devastation. All of it is part of the process. As renowned author J.K. Rowling so eloquently put it "It is impossible to live without failing at something, unless you live so cautiously that you might as well not have lived at all, in which case you have failed by default."

The very same Michael Jordan who won a championship ring was cut from his high school basketball team in 1978. Steven Spielberg was rejected by the University of Southern California School of Cinematic Arts (multiple times). Oprah Winfrey was publicly fired from her first television job. Sidney Poitier flubbed his lines during his first major audition. Walt Disney was fired from the *Kansas City Star* because his editor felt he "lacked imagination and had no good ideas."

I'm a big fan of Denzel Washington. He is an extraordinary actor who has worked hard and achieved a stellar representation in his industry and his statement about failure is one that never ceases to inspire me. I'm certain it will do the same for you. Here's what Denzel says: "You will fail at some point in your life, accept it. You will lose, you will embarrass yourself, you will suck at something…And when you fall throughout life, remember this, fall forward." So, fall, get up, try harder, fall again, and, all the while, remember that every time you fall, you're creating greater forward momentum into greatness.

CHAPTER 21

CAUGHT BETWEEN A ROCK AND A GUY THEY CALLED TANK

Nothing was more demeaning than being plowed over by a guy they called "Tank." At 6-foot, 6-inches and 340 pounds, Tank towered over me. Talk about being caught between a rock and a hard place. I had achieved the goal I set for myself – the goal of being promoted to varsity – yet there I was, face-down on the muddy ground, staring up at a Panzer of a player wondering how I'd gotten myself into such an impossible predicament.

The well-built Fat Albert was standing between me and my dream. Granted, I'd officially made the team, but I had no interest in coasting through the remainder of the season. I wanted to prove to Coaches Russo, Clemens and Montgomery that they'd been right about my potential. I wanted to exceed expectations. I didn't want to keep ending up flat on my ass with the Tank glowering down at me and my older, bigger, brawnier teammates smirking at my lack of aptitude.

Most of us will experience Tank encounters throughout our lives, especially if we're committed to a life of striving and success. We will be running full-out, straight ahead, only to come face-to-face with some obstacle that is seemingly impossible to move through.

Think of Tank as a wall standing in front of you and you'll immediately begin to identify tank after tank in your life – past, present, and future. Each day, we encounter Tanks. They wake up beside us. They sit next to us on our drives to work. They want to date us. They don't want to date us.

As much as the impossible attempts to distract you from holding true to your goals, the sense that you can or should allow yourself to be stopped by an obstacle is only ever an illusion.

I'm not saying you can plow through the immovable walls that life erects in front of you. Some circumstances can't be changed. Some barriers are immune to your efforts to break through, dismantle, or vault over them. Yet, there is always something we can do. Too many times, we see these walls and stop without realizing that we could go around them or choose an alternate path, without seeing the doors that are available to walk through. We don't realize that the only insurmountable walls are the ones we erect within ourselves, and then they're only insurmountable if we allow them to be.

For me, Tank was a wall. Although he didn't come right out and say it, the message he emitted was *If you really want to get to be one of us varsity guys, you must come through me.*

People like Tank play a vital part in "The System." They force you to either become a master of "The System" or to be mastered by "The System." They knock you down, push you off course, and derail you. They are also our greatest teachers. Figuring out ways to get past them will be among the most rewarding moments in your life.

My Uncle Bill once said to me, "If there is a wall that is placed between you and your dream, it's up to you to get to your dream." He instructed me to take a good look at each wall that life put in my path. If a wall was too high to climb, I'd need to try to get around it. If the sides were too long to go around, it was up to me to get a shovel and begin digging underneath it.

"What if none of that works?" I asked him.

He looked at me with a knowing smirk. "Well, Kevin, then you take a few deep breaths, bow your head, and run straight through that son-of-a-bitch. Never let anything stand between you and your dreams!"

Dreams without goals are just dreams. Goals without purpose, or well thought out plans, die before they're ever born. I was fortunate enough to have been taught this by male mentors who cared enough about me that, despite my distractibility – or perhaps because of it – they repeated these lessons until they became ingrained in my brain.

The week after Dayton Roth scored on us, the unsuspecting not-so-Mighty-in-that-moment Teddies was the first week I didn't practice with the other freshmen (except the ones who'd also been elevated to varsity), the first week I wouldn't be playing in the freshmen game.

As a member of the freshman squad, I'd been unstoppable. Now that I'd moved up, success was far from a foregone conclusion. I was out of my element, as anyone is when striving for greatness. With each new benchmark reached and each new crossroad arrived at, there will be growing pains. The pace of varsity practices was much faster, the drills were harder, my teammates were larger, and the time spent explaining was less. A lot less. The other varsity freshmen and I were thrust into the center of the action. It was sink or swim. I didn't question this. I thrived on it. I'd long since decided to put my faith in my coaches. I trusted them, and that trust had yielded results. I'd gotten better as a player. I went from knowing nothing about football to understanding the rules and strategies of the game. I'd memorized the playbook, improved my conditioning, and acquired ever increasing metrics for assessing my performance.

I'd become a much better player, and I'd been elevated to a higher status because of the level of mastery I'd achieved. Now, I had a chance to prove myself within a level of play that was greater, where the stakes were higher. And there was the Tank standing in my way.

I believe that the better the competition you're up against, the more you're forced to perform at a higher level. My experience has borne this out. Almost immediately after beginning to practice with the big guys, my game became elevated. I developed newfound speed. The only times I slowed down were the times I ran into Tank, the human wall. I thought about all those who came before me, the many men and boys the Tank had flattened with his presence. When they were faced with how hard he was going to hit them, and how bad they were going to feel afterwards, had they stood their ground or run scared?

The day Coach instructed me to shift from my middle guard position and line up directly across from Tank, I couldn't look him in the eyes, but I could feel the heat from his breath. The hairs inside my shoulder pads stood on end. My heart pounded. I assumed the three-point stance, my right hand cocked, ready for my patented head slap.

When the ball was snapped, Tank held me to my position. He could've felled me, but he didn't make the effort. That was the thing about Tank. He may've been imposing, but he was also not about to expend any more effort than necessary. Not during practice. Not when the stakes were low. The stakes were never low for me. Since the day I stepped onto Grace A. Green Field, I had given 110% every time out.

"Don't be a hero," Tank told me. "You push me around a bit, I'll push you back, we'll both look like we're doing our job, and nobody has to get hurt." (By "nobody," he meant me).

As much as I wish I could say that I didn't let up but immediately faced off against him with the same level of irreverent investment I brought to my friend David's home years later, I didn't. Obviously, I had no interest in getting pummeled but nor did I want to phone in my performance. Nevertheless, Tank was huge, older and so imposing that, even now, I recoil at the memory of his massive frame. I knew that, if I played full-out, getting hurt would be inevitable.

I took Tank's advice.

The Panzer and I each performed our jobs with the half-assed, lackluster commitment of those who'd rather be safe than sorry. That's a dangerous phrase, by the way. I'm not saying it's not good to keep one's self safe in the face of actual, verifiable danger, but so many of us hold back out of unwarranted fear when we should be playing full-out. As much as my fear may have seemed warranted to my scrawny, freshman self, it wasn't. Getting plowed down by a fellow player wouldn't have been nearly as catastrophic as giving up on myself simply because I was too chicken shit to risk a few temporary falls on the way to becoming the kind of player who'd have made my coaches proud.

A few plays went by. Coach Montgomery called me over to the sideline.

"You have two choices," he said. "Either go back and knock Tank on his big fat butt or give that jersey to someone who really wants to wear it."

Since first setting foot on the field as an imposter, I'd gained close to ten pounds and mastered my patented head slap, but Tank was still twice my size – so big, in fact, that I couldn't envision a scenario in which I'd be able to reach his helmeted head, let alone slap it. I would have to take him on head-on. As I ran back to the huddle, I felt as if I were at a high school dance, about to approach the most beautiful girl in the room, someone like Pam Jones, and ask her to dance while knowing she'd say no and I'd be publicly humiliated. The whole team was about to see me rejected and dejected. Yet, if I didn't at least try, I'd be disappointed in myself.

I ran up to the line, head-to-head with the wall between me and my dreams. My whole body began to tremble. Even my left butt cheek began to shake. The cadences of our team quarterback rang loud and clear through the ear holes in my helmet.

"Hut One! Hut two!" Herb Smith shouted. "3-47! 3-47! Hut, hut!"

There went the ball. I took off. With every ounce of strength, I could muster, I rammed my forearm into the chest of the man they called "Tank." He never saw it coming. Truth be told, I never saw it coming either. I was reacting on instinct. I had worked too hard and come too far to lose the things I wanted most.

When the dust settled, I looked down and there, in the middle of Grace A. Green practice field, lay the unsuspecting giant, lying, unmoving, on the ground as if he were asleep. It took a few seconds for him to blink his eyes open and when he did, they were wide and unsuspecting. No one had ever dropped the big man before.

"Shit Fire!" Coach Montgomery yelled. Although he'd often used the same patented expression to convey to a player "you really @#! this up," at that moment I understood that he meant, "Way to go, Kevin. Good job!"

Coach had asked, and I had delivered. I'd walked up to the most beautiful girl at the dance, issued my invitation, and she'd said "YES!"

Of course, she'd said yes. I was a Mighty Teddy. I was a warrior.

Coach Montgomery let out a second "Shit fire!"

Still basking in the moment, I looked over at the sideline, ready to exchange a smile, but the expression on his face wasn't one of praise, but of warning.

My feet left the ground. My shoulder pads climbed up above my neck and got caught somewhere around my ears. I could feel the flesh being slowly ripped from my body. Not only had Tank reinstated his position, he'd returned the favor. The sleeping giant had awoken, risen from the dusty part of the practice field, and charged at me. I'd knocked him down, and he'd damn near knocked me out of my uniform. When I came to, I hurt in places I'd never hurt before.

In practice, Tank had always behaved as a gentle giant, but that day I gave him a reason to be something different. He tapped into his power and potential and, although his doing so landed me flat on my back, I understood that we both won that day – individually and together.

To this day, I can't remember Tank's given name. But I'll never forget the powerful lesson that knocking each other down imparted. I know I got a lucky shot in on Tank that day, and I paid a heavy and painful price for my short-lived success. But I believe that how we engage with the Tanks that stand in our way has a direct impact on whether we successfully navigate "The System."

When the going gets tough, the tough get going, said the writing on the locker room wall.

Even as I scraped myself off the ground, I felt a sense of triumph. Never mind that, in going head-to-head, all out with Tank, my worst fear had been realized. I'd played to win, and I'd done what I'd have always believed impossible if I'd lacked the courage to try. When the pressure is on and walls are placed before them, great competitors thrive, whereas those who have convinced themselves that losing is okay will always fear the Tanks in their lives too much to face them. Or maybe they will face them, get knocked down and lie there, face down in the dirt, without getting up and trying again.

I believe that most of the pressures in life are self-inflicted. That doesn't mean we should avoid high-pressure situations. In fact, pressure often arises when we're pursuing our passions.

It was my choice to be out there on the field, which meant that it was my choice to put myself in a position to face off against Tank. Or not. I could've sized him up then returned to Coach Montgomery, forfeited my new practice jersey and my spot-on varsity and gone back to playing with the freshman team. I could've abandoned my dream of being one of the guys in the nice practice uniforms. But I didn't. I plowed forward and I did so without knowing what would happen.

If you take responsibility for your life, stand up for yourself, overcome the negative conversation within, work harder and smarter, you'll exceed your wildest expectations. Walls will always be there, and there'll always be Tanks in your life who make the momentarily tempting suggestion that you do only the minimum that's required and never strive for more. But if you give into the temptation to give up, you'll miss out. I say attempt the impossible. You'll be surprised how many walls you knock down.

Truth be told, I was as amazed as everyone else when Tank hit the ground. But the experience did wonders for my self-confidence and enabled me to break through fear. Never mind that Tank proceeded to flatten me. If I could drop a guy that massive, what could I do to a guy my own size?

The moments when we must do battle with the Tanks of this world are what enable us to move beyond our limits and discover that we're far more capable than we know. That doesn't mean you need to go through life recklessly running into walls. Instead, you can go around them, or over them, or tunnel underneath them. Just so long as you don't let them stop you. Obstacles must be handled, quickly or slowly, they must be handled. Stick to what you know – the fundamentals – and concentrate on the task at hand. Block out whatever you're afraid might happen and reflect on everything you've done to get you to this point, and everything you stand to gain by continuing onward. Remember all the hard work, the hours of practice, and accumulated wins that've gotten you to where you are. Put your confidence back where it belongs – in yourself and your abilities. Then, look Tank straight in his eyes and knock him on his butt. Only, after you do, don't get so lost in self-congratulations that you neglect to watch your back.

"You can never prove you are the best at something, unless you've proved it in competition," my Uncle Bill once told me, as we watched one of his star high school basketball players work out during a practice. My Uncle Bill was a basketball coach at another city school and was always taking me to see his competitors' games so he could scout the competition. He knew what it took to excel on the court and in life. He understood that winners are created only when they're playing a high-stakes game, when they recognize that there's no such thing as taking it easy. Whether it be in practice or in a championship game, we always need to be doing whatever will enable us to elevate our game.

People like Tank are an incentive to performing at our highest level, which in turn better equips us to play all-out when it matters. Let's celebrate the Tanks of this world. And let's celebrate the versions of ourselves we must become to knock them down. The next time I knocked a teammate on his back side, I stood over him to see if he was going to get up, then I looked him in the eye and told him I'd be knocking him on his butt all day long. I've continued to live my life that way, facing obstacles head-on and not letting or giving up.

I'm lucky that I learned to play football surrounded by winners. My coaches and teammates repeatedly taught me, by example and explanation, that, if you have a winning mindset, there's no room for excuses. In fact, excuses only sound good to the person that are making them. Even then, when you're committed to living as a winner, you'll call bullshit on yourself. If you're committed to adopting a winning mentality, you must be willing to pay the price. You must make sacrifices and work overtime to get your body and mind fully prepared to take all the hard hits that come your way. Navigating through life as someone who delivers on their potential, even if it means they sometimes get knocked on their ass, has made me tougher. I'm sure that, when you look at your life and consider the situations you've triumphed over, you'll see how the winning moments in your past, even if they were challenging or painful at the time, made you stronger. String a couple of these victories together and you'll see that you were – and are – more capable than you ever believed.

The Tanks in our lives are blessings. Without them, we'd never face our fears. We'd never know the pride filled exhilaration of getting to the next level. I go through life each day excited for any impossible walls and immovable obstacles that stand between me and the realization of my dreams and I encourage those around me to do the same. I'd challenge you to adopt a similar outlook. The next time you're caught between a rock and a hard place, use a Tank to get you moving.

CHAPTER 22

DON'T QUIT, IF YOU STILL WANT TO PLAY

All the weeks were hard, but the week after we played Dayton Roth was the hardest. It wasn't just being on the varsity squad that made it challenging. Coach Montgomery was on a mission. Never mind that we'd already slogged through mud and rain, extreme heat, the Bull in the Middle, wind sprints, and tip drills, this particular week, he was determined to show us that winners worked harder after losses. He was determined not to let the upcoming game end up like the previous one. There came a point during every practice when I couldn't feel my legs. Fatigue set in. I watched the other players, most of whom I'd always perceived as tougher than I was, and from the expressions on their faces I could tell that they were on the verge of breaking down. Some did break down. They cried out for mercy or slunk over to the sidelines where they sat, shivering from cold and shame.

Coach was relentless. I don't know many people who could have put up with the demands he placed upon us. As he egged us on, inspiring us to greatness with drills designed to push us so far out of our comfort zones that we could barely breathe, he reminded us that only cowards were quitters. He said we'd beaten ourselves during our battle with Dayton Roth. Oh, how the mighty had fallen. He wasn't about to let that happen again.

As a child, Pops worked in a cotton field to help put food on his family's table. Whenever he recalled all the hard work that required, he'd remind me that fatigue drained you of the will to go on, giving your opponent the one up on you, robbing you of the ability to use your precious skills, throwing your rhythm and coordination off, and separating you from what you desired most.

Coach Montgomery wanted us fatigued. He wanted us on the verge of breaking down so we could practice producing extraordinary results under the most demanding circumstances. He was hell-bent that his team was not going to get conquered, and he was teaching us that practicing under the hardest, harshest conditions would equip us to excel during game-time and to make games seem almost easy by comparison. This is a time-tested, effective, old school strategy.

The physical rigor wasn't the only thing that was getting to us. We had gone from the heat to mud and rain, to a sudden drop in the temperature. We were now practicing in single digit weather, with hands as cold as icicles.

Why else would marathoners train at high altitudes or medical students subject themselves to the grueling residency shifts? By doing the things that need to be done in the most rigorous of conditions, we acquire the capacity to overcome any obstacles.

Nothing I had done up to that point had prepared me for the cold. For the first time since I joined the team, I began to second-guess my resolve. Why was I doing this? Was it worth it? I had a tough time getting my head into the game. Every time I tackled someone; I was more worried about getting hurt than getting ahead.

In this book to this point, I've focused a lot on internal conditions, on the attitudes and actions that separate winners from their less effective counterparts, but external circumstances matter too. Many times, we face conditions that are uncontrollable and unavoidable. Yes, there will be snow, rain, and ice, and there will also be illness, death, divorce, infidelity and all sorts of events that are outside our capacity to control. How we react to these circumstances is a testament not only to our characters, but to our conditioning. By developing our values and living life stringing together victory after hard-won victory, by implementing the fundamentals into our daily lives, we become so resilient that although we may experience moments of wanting to give up, we never do. We're too practiced in the art of preparation and too enlivened by our passions to let ourselves be derailed by life's inevitable discomforts.

All I'd learned about myself, the sacrifices I'd made, everything was now on the line as Coach Montgomery pushed me to go farther than I thought possible. I was exhausted, freezing, operating at the limits of my capacity, and wishing desperately for it all to be over. My only saving grace was that, in the back of my mind, I knew that whatever I was doing would help me and my teammates be better prepared for our next game. I tried to remind myself that running back and forth was keeping what little of me could still move warm.

The others were equally spent. Their shoulders slumped. Their cleats churned up the earth with steely resolve rather than the typical excitement. It was drudgery. There are moments when, in the relentless pursuit of a goal worth attaining, the best you can do is put your head down and trudge forward. There will be days when fun eludes you. That's okay. Keep going anyway.

There are only so many things in "The System" of life that you have no control over, and the weather is one of those uncontrollable forces you must deal with. As I look back on the hardest week of my high school football career, I believe that only the best-conditioned players can conquer the bitter cold. When Mother Nature cops an attitude, the person who is mentally and physically ready to face whatever comes their way will emerge triumphant. This may have been Coach Montgomery's line of thinking. I can't say for certain. I know he was doing his utmost to toughen us up. I don't believe he was purposely trying to break us, even though I watched many of my teammates fall, one by one. Amid this dropping-like-flies phenomenon, I started to notice who the cold had beaten. None of the starters gave up. They ran play after play, blowing the winter air into their hands and yelling out like they were enjoying being out in the elements. I found my courage in them. The weather was going to be what it was going to be. Complaining wouldn't get me anywhere except on the sidelines with those of my teammates who had given up and given in, relinquishing their greatness in the face of discomfort. That wouldn't be me.

I made up my mind to stop thinking so much about how cold I was and keep my head on what I could control – doing my best at the job at hand. I was still cold, but I quickly discovered that yelling gave me some pleasure and provided a much-needed distraction.

I forgot about going inside and getting out of the cold and remained fixed on staying on the field. I wanted to be the last man standing. I wasn't. Yes, there were those who quit – a handful of second stringers who got going when the going got tough. But the rest of us refused to drop. We were a team. A unit. We were the Mighty Teddies and we refused to give up on ourselves or each other.

I blew into my hands. I yelled like a wild animal. I started to have fun every time I got hit or hit somebody. I yelled louder. I got warmer.

Everyone thinks about quitting. Not everyone quits. When I was a freshman in college, my circumstances got hard. My girlfriend at the time got pregnant and I had to hurry up and take responsibility. Luckily, I found a passage that I read every day to get myself through. I hope these words will resonate with you, as they did with me.

"Don't Quit," Author Unknown.

When things go wrong, as they sometimes will;
When the road you're trudging seems all up hill;
When funds are low and the debts are high,
And you want to smile, but you have to sigh;
When cares are pressing you down a bit,
Rest if you must, but don't you quit.

Life is queer with its twist and turns,
As every one of us sometimes learns;
And many a person turn about,
When they might have won had they stuck it out.
So, don't give up though the pace seems slow
You may succeed with another blow.

Often the struggler has given up,
When he might have captured the victor's cup;
And he learned too late when your hardest hit,
It's when things seem worst, that you mustn't quit.

When it comes to striving for your heart's desires, know that quitting your quest is tantamount to quitting yourself. Even if you give up taking action in the direction you want to go, there will be no giving up self-recrimination. You'll be the one who'll have to live with the reruns that will keep playing back in your mind. The *what ifs*, *if onlys,* and *I could've beens* will stack up inside of you like Dominoes, crashing down upon each other.

I stayed on that field that day, surrounded by my diehard teammates, each of us refusing to succumb to the lure of mediocrity, and we were each better for it.

CHAPTER 23

THE EDGE

Nobody ever said life as a Mighty Teddy was going to be easy, but nor had anyone warned me how hard I'd be expected to work. Other than my mother packing up and leaving town without us, the week of practice following the Dayton Roth game and leading up to the Dayton Patterson game was the hardest thing I'd ever experienced. I was cold, tired and sore. At night, after practice, I'd get home and the voice of Coach Montgomery would echo in my head.

When my alarm clock shrilled me awake in the morning, I'd swear it was his whistle and spring out of bed ready for another round of wobbly-legged, exhausted wind sprints. Sure, I'd dug deep and played hard, refusing to succumb to exhaustion, and proving to myself and my team, day in and day out, that they could depend on me, but the thing about "The System" is that, although successes can and often do build upon each other, there can be no resting on your previous accomplishments, just as there can be no half-assing it. We were expected to exhibit all the effort we could muster. I thought I'd been working hard before, and I had been, but now that I'd made it to varsity – and especially now that I'd made it to varsity after our first and only loss of the season – the level of expected performance went beyond anything I'd ever experienced. Each day, I was outperforming my previous day's self, exhibiting more than I'd believed myself capable of.

When your body is at its max with pain, your mind must work overtime to remind you how tough you really are. That was something I didn't realize until I experienced it firsthand. At the end of the day, winning is a mind game. The attainment of one's dreams is a mind game. Once the body is sufficiently conditioned that it is available for peak performance, being able to outshine everyone else, and your former self, becomes an issue of mental fortitude.

Constantly playing in your head are thoughts, which are essentially mental messages. We can train the brain just as we train the body, and this is done by working out our mindset. Now that I teach cognitive training, I tell my clients that we can convince our minds of anything. Using cognitive processes, we can develop what I refer to as "callouses of the mind." In this way, mental resilience makes the seemingly impossible possible. Sometimes, you must perform at your best when you are feeling your worst. You can be sick, hurt, emotionally off-kilter, stressed, or struggling with outside life circumstances, yet your head needs to be in the game. Excuses don't count. When your number is called, nobody cares if you're sick, tired, or having a bad day, you've got to be ready to rush onto the field and give it your all.

There are always going to be those times when you'd rather be doing something other than what's necessary. But the people who rise to and remain at the top don't avoid life's challenges. When their number is called, they stand up and get counted, whereas others don't and then act surprised when they're counted out. As a Mighty Teddy, I was having drilled into my very cells that, no matter what, I needed to hold true to the program and remain mentally tough. That toughness, I was discovering, would get me through anything with my dreams not only intact but even more achievable than ever.

Coach Montgomery wasn't trying to break us. He was seeing what we were made of. And he was teaching us how to tap into potential we didn't know we had. He saw more power and potential in us than we saw within ourselves and that week he was inviting us to access it. When everything is perfect, confidence, enthusiasm, and positivity come easily.

When every part of your body wants to give up and you muster up the ability to keep working toward your goals, that's when you find out who you really are. That's when you're unstoppable.

"The System" will always toss adversity at you. Whether you're faced with the goal of writing a book that will keep young people motivating themselves, rather than waiting to be motivated, or you're trying to show a 15-year-old pregnant girl why it is good for her unborn baby to be brought into this world when she's nothing but a child herself, there will inevitably be obstacles and opportunities.

Don't get the wrong idea. "The System" is not out to get you. But to succeed at life, you must grow, and to grow you must be challenged, sometimes to the point of feeling as if the obstacles before you are insurmountable. It's what you do under suboptimal circumstances that determines whether you will win or lose. That's not to say that those who strive to win won't suffer occasional losses, or that those who have resigned themselves to a lifetime of loss might not experience the occasional victory. But it's the aggregate moments of the combined crossroads in our life that, when added together, determine whether we are "winners" or "losers." After a demoralizing loss and in the face of subpar conditions, and drill after punishing drill, we had to dig deep into our physical and mental reserves.

That week's practice was a huge confidence builder. I learned that once you know you can fight a great battle out in the freezing cold, and practice harder and longer than you'd have believed possible, you gain a huge edge over your competition. No one can take that away from you.

No matter how much you think you have suffered, or how much you think you have sacrificed, you are capable of triumphing over more than you can conceive. It can be tempting to think your struggles are worse than everyone else's, yet I can assure you that, no matter what circumstances you find yourself up against, now or in the future, and no matter what your past, there are hundreds of others who have suffered and sacrificed more. I don't mean this to be pessimistic, but rather to point to the resilience that we human beings exhibit.

One of my clients, Mr. Robert Kay, whom I admire and respect, once told me that suffering was a choice. He refused to give up after adversity because, as he put it, "it's character building." I was with him when he got a call that the mother of his two children had been diagnosed with cancer during a routine doctor's visit. Robert didn't panic. He simply accepted the news and did what had to be done. She died 30 days after she learned the news and he went on to honor her memory and be the best parent he could be to their children. He never allowed himself to wallow in self-pity and he strove to be an example of her living legacy.

Whatever you face, or whatever you've already faced, if you cannot just make it through but move through it with faith and perseverance, you'll not only have mastered "The System," you'll have achieved mastery over yourself.

CHAPTER 24

NEVER-FORGOTTEN THURSDAY

Anyone who entered the two oversized double doors of the entranceway to Roosevelt High School couldn't help but notice the symbol of the Mighty Teddies that rested in the middle of the hallway floor. A full-grown grizzly bear wearing a bright red shirt on that said the Mighty Teddies was painted onto the floor with enamel paint. Coach Clemens, who taught art in addition to coaching football, had painted it with some of the students, and it was a testament to our institutional pride. School spirit and a rich tradition of history rested on the shoulders of this painted not-so-cuddly bear. Often, this monument to greatness would be carefully guarded by some proud student who had made it his or her duty to protect this badge of honor.

If you were one of the unlucky few who accidentally or deliberately walked over this symbol of greatness, this volunteer protector of the school's honor would give you an immediate lesson in school spirit – a lesson that only ever had to be taught once.

Thursday evening practices were another ritualized reminder of Roosevelt High School spirit. It was the time when the coaches would pass out the white mesh game jerseys I'd been coveting. Each week I'd watched this ritual, and each week I'd wished those who wore these hallowed jerseys Godspeed and luck. Leading up to being pulled up to the varsity squad, I often wondered what it would feel like to be one of the chosen few who walked the hallways of our school while being worshipped and revered. Back in the day, football players were the only ones who could wear the same clothes twice in a row without anyone saying anything about it!

Before being promoted to varsity, I'd held one of the jerseys once. It wasn't exactly the reverent experience I'd dreamed about, considering I picked it up off the locker room floor.

Larry Hightower was getting dressed when his jersey fell out of his locker. I stooped down retrieved it and handed it to him. That was it. Still, for the moment I held it, I felt as if I were holding the history of all those who had played before.

Each jersey was a symbol of what being Number One was about. I could imagine myself wearing one while walking the hallways of Roosevelt High on game day, with all eyes on me.

I'd been so proud as a high school student, so reverent and full of awe. I never imagined that anyone else, let alone anyone I loved deeply, would have anything other than a phenomenal high school experience. But on Thursday, October 2, 1997, I found myself standing at the entrance of my oldest daughter's school, wondering where it had all gone wrong. Perhaps, if my daughter felt about Belmont High the way I'd felt about Roosevelt High School and the Mighty Fighting Teddies, she wouldn't be in danger of failing and I wouldn't have had to fly almost 500 miles to spend a week following her from one class to another. Roosevelt High had closed going into my junior year. She was attending Belmont, where kids didn't seem possessed of the same academic and athletic fervor that I remembered from my own pre-collegiate days. I wasn't sure if that was a result of the differences between the schools, or a sign of the times. Either way, as I parted the mighty doors of this public high school, my attention was drawn to their symbol of school spirit, their seal, which I knew reflected many years of pride and tradition. No one was guarding it. Whatever fantasies I'd entertained about triumphant high school moments were quickly erased by the sight of those who walked the hallowed halls of this institution. It was 6:45 a.m. The cries of a child reverberated through the narrow corridor. A child in a high school? My attention was drawn to the wailing infant who was accompanied by a young girl who I could only assume was her mother. The teen couldn't have been older than fourteen or fifteen. Before I could fully register my shock, I noticed that she wasn't the only student striding down the hallway with a child in tow.

There were others with children not quite ready to be walking the hallways of a nursery, let alone the hallways of a high school. I wasn't sure whether to be dismayed or encouraged. Perhaps, both? These young mothers could've used their circumstances to give up on themselves and fail to realize their educational potential, yet they continued coming to school with the purpose of beating the odds and getting an education. Whatever they'd done, or hadn't done, they refused to quit. It was a powerful reminder to me, whose own child was somewhere inside the school, that it was possible to pursue one's dreams while simultaneously taking care of a child you were too young to have.

Many times, I'd wished I'd been better equipped to be a parent when my daughter came along. With her, I'd had to learn on the playing, as opposed to the practice, field. As a result, I lacked skill and preparation.

A cacophony of voices rang out from down the hall, loud and aggressive. It wasn't a fight song. It was the sound of disrespect. My eyes bugged as I heard a young white youth address a black youth with a cheerily uttered N-word and receive a high five instead of a fist to the face. There wasn't even a reprimand.

I turned around 360 degrees to fully take in the unfamiliar surroundings. The young people who came in were dressed in attire unlike anything I'd ever seen before. Many of them had earrings in their noses and eyebrows. One youth appeared to be almost completely covered in tattoos.

The teachers, who were interspersed with their students, looked weighted down with the burden of molding the minds of those who appeared not to have a thought in their stubborn heads. The frustration showed on the faces of those who were responsible for the development of these misguided souls, and I thought about the educators I'd admired and respected when I was in high school. I felt sorry for the teachers at Belmont. I was certain they'd gotten into teaching to make an impact on impressionable youth, yet that wasn't what seemed to be happening.

Later, sitting in history class with my daughter, I observed her teacher, Mr. Roger, a young enthusiastic dreamer. I could tell immediately that he had the best of intentions and was deeply invested in every student. Unfortunately, many of the messages he was attempting to deliver routinely fell by the wayside of those empty-minded young people who sat around his room. Not to say that all those in his class were lost causes, but many of them wore expressions that clearly conveyed they would've rather been doing their nails, or talking about last night's score, than paying attention to what the teacher was writing on the blackboard.

Say what you mean, and mean what you say, Mr. Roger wrote.

As I watched him, still willing to cast his reel of hope after what must've been days, weeks, months (maybe even years) of coming up empty, the thought ran through my head that Mr. Roger was a winner. I could almost hear a fight song playing in the background. He was determined to reach his students and although, indeed, many of them appeared disinterested and lackadaisical, several began leaning forward in their chairs, attentive despite the "uncoolness" of the subject matter. Unlike so many of his contemporaries, Mr. Roger refused to give up. He later told me that, although he tried to get through to all his classes, the one I attended with my daughter was one of the best, if not the best. I was proud to hear these words. His was one of the few classes, and he was one of the few teachers, my daughter liked.

With *Say what you mean and mean what you say* prominently scrawled on the board, Mr. Roger went on to talk about the report he'd received from the substitute teacher who filled in for him one day when he was absent. He explained, in very simple terms, how his class was structured. It was divided into half-hour sessions, one before lunch, the second half of the class after. He looked meaningfully around the room as the students squirmed in their seats. It wasn't long before I realized why they were so uncomfortable. Mr. Roger said that the report he'd gotten from the sub was that the students would show up for the first part of class, then fail to return for the second half.

"I don't know what happened between the two floors that separate the classroom from the lunchroom," he said. "Maybe the maps we handed out at the beginning of the school year were somehow incorrect. I wouldn't be surprised, with all the typos that are in them. A lot like the information in some of the textbooks they give us to work with. But –" He looked from student to student, his gaze imbued with meaning. "We've been making it through for almost a year now. Why wait till now to get lost?"

I was trying to figure out where he was going with his coy form of confrontation. This guy had just written *Say what you mean and mean what you say.* So why was he beating around the bush? Why not say what he meant and be done with it? I come from an in-your-face, deal-direct, football-oriented approach, a confrontational, tough-love communication style.

I followed his gaze around the room, studying the expressions on the students' faces. What, exactly, was Mr. Roger attempting to convey? Then, the teacher's speech took an unexpected twist. He launched into a story. He told the students (and me) that he'd recently been sitting in an eatery with friends when they began making disparaging remarks about the public-school system and his job as a teacher. They felt he would do better, and would be more appreciated, in the private school system.

He said that he'd protested vehemently, telling his friends that he was making a difference and that Belmont High School wasn't deserving of its bad rap. He launched into an impassioned speech about how special his students were and how they'd been unfairly underestimated. His voice swelled with pride as he talked about his students and just how much potential they possessed. Midway through his impassioned address, however, Mr. Roger looked up and noticed that the television that was over the table where he and his friends were sitting showed a lead story on the evening news, which featured Belmont High. On screen, one of the students whose potential he'd just proclaimed was being placed into the back seat of a police cruiser. He said his whole evening had been spoiled by that report.

He held a book high over his head. "This is the reason they give you books that have misspelled words in them and outdated material. The Dayton City School System thinks you won't notice that Ronald Regan's name is spelled Reagan in the books. They think you don't care about yourselves or your future, so why should they care about your education? The problem here –" He let the book fall to the floor with a dramatic thud. "–is that I care." He began to walk around the room, from desk to desk, "The only bright spot is that all the young ladies somehow found their way back for the second session." As he walked, he stopped in front of each of the five young men that had cut his class. "I guess that's because, if women are given a map, they read it." He made each young man read the quote on the blackboard and give his definition of what he thought it meant.

One young man studied it for a minute before answering in broken English. "Ah, it's like, you know, you've got to back what you said, like selling wolf tickets."

Mr. Roger took a moment before he replied. "You could look at it that way. What about you?" he asked another.

The second student took the easy way out. "It's just what he'd said." He pointed to the young man who'd gone before him.

The class laughed, but Mr. Roger didn't get the humor. He faced outward to address not only those who'd cut, but the rest of the class as well. "That quote on the board says that your words must reflect your actions. For every time a kid cuts my class or fails to return for the second part of the session, I take it as a personal attack against me."

Mr. Roger took the responsibility of educating young people seriously. He was proud to be a teacher at Belmont, and, when he confronted his students, he was letting them know both that he loved them and that they had let him down.

This is important.

Letting people off the hook isn't loving at all. Instead, it conveys a message that you've given up on them. You believe them to be capable of nothing more than mediocrity.

"You, too, should take great pride in the school," Mr. Roger said. "Belmont High School will become a permanent tattoo that you'll wear for the rest of your life. You can drop out today, and Belmont will be the school you dropped out of. Be an honor student, and you're an honor student of Belmont High. This school will be with you forever. You can't go through life expecting to gain anything, if you've only given a half-hearted performance. You have to do the whole program."

"Why?" one student asked.

"The more effort, the more intense your feelings will be about the things you do, your job, your school, your life. The more intense you are, the more committed you are. The more pride you have, the less likely you are to let yourself down, and the more you will mean to others."

I was so deeply impressed with Mr. Roger's commitment to his students and himself that I half wished I had a Mighty Teddies jersey to give him. I said a silent prayer of thanks for those who had believed enough in me to push me to be greater than I believed possible.

Coach Montgomery had instilled in all of us players the firmly held conviction that words and actions mattered. Or maybe it wasn't that he instilled it in us so much as that he recruited and retained only those who said what they meant and meant what they said.

I said I wanted to be one of those guys in the nice practice jerseys, and I meant it enough to do whatever I had to get to the next level and stay there. I said I'd never let my coaches down and, aside from a brief moment of letting up before bravely facing (and temporarily felling) Tank, I stuck by that commitment.

As I sat beside my daughter, listening to Mr. Roger speak, I was transported back to a memory that remained as fresh that day as if it were happening.

I could still hear my name as it echoed through the locker room (as Mr. Roger's words did, when he delivered his message to his class).

"McLemore!" yelled Coach Montgomery.

For a moment, I was too stunned to react. Larry Hightower, our star running back, snapped his fingers in front of my face, bringing me out of shock and back into reality. "You forget your name?"

Coach yelled out again. "Ain't got all day son. Get in here!"

As I walked over to the equipment room, Coach Montgomery sat there holding a white game day jersey. With a stern expression, he tossed it at me. I stood there as if my feet were planted in the mud. The jersey fell from my face into my hands.

Before I could say "Thanks," Coach said, "Don't miss the bus, son."

Then, he began the typical Thursday ritual, handing out the jerseys to the other players, like what had just happened wasn't a big deal. Even though at that moment I felt as if I'd been singled out for greatness, there were a couple of my freshman peers who got their varsity game jerseys, too, including Jason Kirkland.

Jason was the toughest kid I knew. Because we'd been friends since first grade, people figured I was as tough as he was, so I tried to be. As a teammate, he looked out for me and made sure I understood what I had to do. I never wanted to let him down. Our uplifting brand of competitiveness was one of the reasons I enjoyed the game some much. Sure, I had other teammates, like Larry Lee, that eventually went on to play pro football, but there was no one I'd have rather played with than Jason. We had each other's backs. Not only when we were running from the Chains of Rap Brown, but when we were running toward the end zone.

Coach Montgomery could have handed out forty-four jerseys. As long as Jason and I got one, that was all that mattered. My dream had come true! From the moment I got the red and white jerseys, something inside of me wanted to run out into the street and tell the whole world that, by sticking true to my vow, I'd made what I said I wanted to happen happen. But something held me back. It was like a dark cloud hovering overhead. I looked up from running my fingers across the bright red 67 painted on the jersey and immediately locked eyes with Tank. At first, I thought he had come back to put me down again after my stupid act of bravery during practice. But before I could run, he spoke these words, "The hard part now will be keeping it." With no further explanation, he walked away.

What was that about? I wondered.

I'd done all that had been asked of me – come early, stayed late, survived Bull in the Middle, hustled through wind sprints, and even endured tip drills in single-digit weather. I was a Teddy! I even had the jersey to prove it!

Tank's words were like a Mack truck plowing into my self-congratulatory inward celebration. I hadn't given any thought to the problems and pressures created by newfound victories. I didn't know then what I know now. When you activate your dreams, there will be cheerleaders, yes, but there will also be dream stealers.

I have come to believe that dreams and personal sacrifices go hand in hand, but that, in the end, the rewards when your dreams come true are far sweeter for any bitterness you've endured. If you put the time and effort into reaching your life's goals, in time, your efforts will pay off. Sometimes, they pay off double.

Tank wasn't trying to steal my dreams. He was warning me that it was up to me to hold onto them. I was now officially a Mighty Teddy, which made me the object not just of admiration but of envy.

Tank's warning made me think long and hard about not just what I'd said, but what it meant. Getting the jersey, I'd wanted and getting promoted to varsity came with a great deal of responsibility that I had never thought about before. Even the worst teams in the city were focused on taking us Teddies down. They centered their entire strategy around dethroning us merely because we'd made it to the top.

I recalled the knowing words of Uncle Bill. "It is harder to stay on top than it is to get there."

As a young black American, I'd had plenty of experience surviving oppression, racism, and other social adversities, but now with this jersey in hand, I was faced with a task for which I had little to no experience. For the first time, I had to survive prosperity.

I've learned over the years that when a person achieves his or her goals, he or she will often realize they're in uncharted territory, and in over their heads. This doesn't mean we shouldn't strive to attain what we say we want. We should. But, once we get there, we need to figure out who we must be and what we must do to stay there (or even to stretch ourselves to achieve the next level of greatness).

Learning how to handle success when it comes is a vital part of effectively navigating "The System." Tank's wise, if ruthlessly delivered, words taught me that I should never brag about myself. Egotism is the anesthetic that numbs the pain of stupidity. After Tank made me aware that I could never take my achievements for granted, I placed a terrific amount of pressure on myself to keep that Mighty Teddies jersey.

Even as a naïve freshman, I knew the value of what Tank, the biggest, baddest offensive guard and defensive tackle, had imparted. I didn't want to be a one-night wonder, nor was I willing to have wished for, and worked for, something, only to have it taken away from me.

I thought *I'll wear my number 67, XXL with the pride and tradition that the Mighty Teddies stand for. I'll run home singing our team's fight song. I'll walk the hallways of Roosevelt High School in my game day jersey and white turtleneck, like the champions that wore the jersey before me. And as much as I would like to go out and tell the world of my great accomplishment, I'll keep my mouth shut, and let my actions speak for themselves.*

CHAPTER 25

PREPARE FOR THE WORST AND THERE'LL BE NO SURPRISES

Less than twenty-four hours after having my number 67 varsity jersey handed to me, I walked through the hallways of Roosevelt High School, a scrawnier, younger version of the players I'd been idolizing from afar. I knew people were staring, but I didn't say anything about my recent rise to greatness. I let the jersey speak for itself.

After school let out, I headed straight to the locker room where, after being the first to finish getting dressed, I stood waiting, both ankles tightly wrapped with tape. My eyes panned the locker room. Most of the other guys were still getting ready. Like me, they'd taken off the turtlenecks they'd worn to school and replaced them with pads, which filled in the space between their jerseys and themselves. I studied Larry Hightower and Tank as they applied black paint under their eyes. Larry Hightower turned and caught me looking. Shoot. I hadn't wanted it to show that I was star struck. My running back idol approached me.

I figured I was in for a hazing ritual, so I held my shoulder pad and braced myself for whatever was to come. To my surprise, Larry had a gift for me. He said he wanted to give me something that had been passed down to him by one of the upperclassmen who came before him. He explained that there was a Mighty Teddy tradition in which an upperclassman gave an item to a new member to the team to wear in their first game. He held out me a pair of old, worn out, forearm pads.

I had a mental flash of all the times he'd run over me, then helped me to my feet so he could run over me again. Each time he'd laughed at my many flattenings, it hadn't been because he enjoyed what he was doing to me, but because he liked me as much as I looked up to him.

"Thank you."

I slipped the forearm pads over my forearms and taped them so they'd stay put. As I walked past the locker room mirror, I got a glimpse of myself. What I saw wasn't just a reflection of a slender black kid in a football uniform. What I saw was everything I'd worked so hard for. It had all been worth it. The exterior door swung open and a blast of frigid air slapped me out of my inward celebration. The weather outside had hit a record low: six degrees below zero. Icy rain fell from an angry, ominous sky. We were about to go out and do battle against Jefferson Township.

So, what if it was sleeting? We were Mighty Teddies. We had been out bravely facing the elements all week – running and jumping, hitting and being hit, When the temperature was a single digit below Zero. Adversity was just part of the game. Part of life. I stood in line to get my red parka with white lettering on the back, and, out of the corner of my eye, I noticed Jason Kirkland slipping his long underwear on under his uniform. I didn't know if this was right or wrong, but I followed suit.

In my eagerness, I'd gotten ready so early that I still had time for a quick undergarment insulation maneuver before the time came to head out to the bus, proudly belting out our fight song. I also put on an extra pair of long socks and my insulated gloves. Moments later, I joined the rest of my teammates and together we walked down the line of singing underclassman. It was a powerful procession. My heartbeat quickened with anticipation.

Even after we boarded the bus, I could hear the muffled sounds of the mighty fight song from outside. But there wasn't a sound being made inside. I'd expected the bus to be a continuation of that excitement. Yet, there was nothing. Silence. I studied the faces of those already on the bus. They were scowling. Somber. There were no songs being sung. No one was even talking. As I took to my seat in the back of the bus (the place where freshmen had to sit), Coach Montgomery boarded. He cleared his throat.

"Adversity is just part of life. If you plan to live in this world, you must learn how to handle it. It builds character. It forces you to analyze yourself, to figure out what's wrong, so, instead of making it worse, you can make it better. We lost a game last week that we should have won. Some would have given up. Some did give up. That's why we have some new faces on the bus tonight and are missing some of the old ones. Those of you who are here today know how to dig deep and play hard. You are Mighty Teddies. I know it's cold out there. The other team will be just as cold. We have a game to play, plain and simple. Another of your teammates is fighting a much bigger battle than the one that's ahead of us right now. Big John William's father died of a brain tumor this morning. Before you take the field tonight, I want you to search your souls, and..."

Before Coach Montgomery could utter another word, Big John boarded the bus, interrupting Coach's speech. Coach stopped his train of thought mid-sentence, interrupting himself before telling John he didn't have to be a hero.

"I'm part of this team," John replied. "And this is where my dad would have wanted me to be."

Unbeknownst to me, many of my teammates had already heard of John's loss. They knew about his struggle and were prepared to rally around him like the stand-up teammates they were. It turned out that, even amid his mourning, Big John didn't want to take from the team, he wanted to give to it. To this day, I'm blown away by the fact that Big John showed up to play the day after his father's death. I'm not sure what I would have done in his situation. I'm not even saying there was a right or wrong thing to do. There was only the choice he made, a choice that revealed his dedication to the Mighty Teddies, to himself, and to his father's memory.

I learned later that John had known his father was dying for some time before Mr. William passed. What I found out what he'd been dealing with, I'd marvel at my teammate's dedication. He came to practice every day and gave his all, just like the rest of us, while knowing that his father wasn't long for this world. My own dad had known about Mr. William's impending death too but had chosen not to tell me. Maybe, he figured it'd effect my play, or maybe he didn't know how to talk about the fact that he was losing his best friend.

Coach Montgomery gave Big John a hug, something I'd never seen him do to any of the players and, when they pulled apart, Coach gave the okay for the driver to pull away and take us to the game.

When he resumed his speech, his tone was more uplifting. "When face to face with adversity, you must act on the situation immediately. The problem won't just go away, so don't try to put it off. Let Big John be an example. Winners treat adversity as a test, not as a threat. Right John?"

"Right!" John yelled back like the mighty warrior that he was.

Big John launched into the team fight song. My voice caught in my throat, emotion surging to the surface, yet I joined in along with everybody else. We merged our voices in solidarity and in memory of Mr. Williams and in support of Big John, who refused to stay down when life knocked him down. He was using his dad's death as a measuring stick to prove to himself what he was made of. We would do the same. We would put our victories and defeats into proper perspective.

Adversity is a given. People will die, they'll leave, they'll let you down. You'll suffer setbacks and losses. It's inevitable. What isn't inevitable is giving up. Even when you are at your lowest point, you have the choice to continue onward, making decisions that will empower you and ensure your progress. Big John couldn't bring his dad back, but he could and would dedicate that night's game to his father.

In the years since I began keeping a journal – which I started around the same time I started football – Uncle Bill, Grandpa Joe, Momma Annie (my grandmother), Coach Tom Clemens, my younger brother Anthony, my baby sister Ronda, my big brother Dwight, my father Leroy, and my Uncle Ron have all passed on. Today, I am living with a concussion which causes me consistent headaches and difficulty retaining new and remembering old information. Yet, none of that is reason to quit.

As I prepare for the second half of my life, I can't help but to remember what my dad said to me two nights before he passed away. First, he said, "I love you," something he had never said to me my whole life. Then, he said he was proud of me, another thing he'd never said. As if that weren't enough, he finished by adding that it's not how you die that matters, but how you live that will make your story worth telling.

"Live great, Kevin," he instructed. "And go write your story."

Dad died on Christmas Eve, 2008, while I was driving from Dayton, Ohio back to Phoenixville, Pennsylvania to be there for my kids on Christmas morning. I'd left, thinking that my father would hold on for long enough for me to return to Dayton and see him one more time. When I got the call, two hours into my drive home to be with my kids on Christmas, telling me that my dad had quietly slipped out of this world, I didn't turn back. I continued driving to Phoenixville, PA, crying all the way.

Some would ask "Why did you leave your father's bed side when you knew he didn't have long?"

My answer is immediate and unwavering. "That's what my father would have wanted me to do."

CHAPTER 26

THE MAIN OBJECTIVE IS SURVIVAL

As I watched Big John run out onto the field, my heart was heavy. There are times when you can't always explain or account for all the adversities you are faced with, either in life or on the playing field. If I hadn't known what he was up against, I'd never have suspected. Big John ran up and down the field of Welcome Stadium as if it were just another game day and the only thing on his mind was winning. I wondered if that was how he really felt or if his exterior was as deceptive as the Astroturf beneath his cleats.

The lawn of the 20th century never needed cutting, never sprouted weeds, and appeared to be perfect and well-kept, but upon closer inspection you'd see it was only an illusion. It wasn't real. If you knelt and felt it, it was like coarse shag carpet, interspersed with needles. It was rough. Big John ran through his warmups like he had nothing on his mind but playing in this game. As I watched, I couldn't help thinking how remarkable he was to have the drive to persevere, regardless of his situation.

Coach Clemens called for the defensive players to line up for tip drill warm-ups: three men up front, three in back to catch the ball. We had worked so hard at tip drills during practice that to do them as a pre-game warm-up felt almost second nature.

The temperature on the bottom of the scoreboard read ten below zero. Freezing rain coated the ground. The tips of my fingers were numb. They hurt every time I touched anything, but I never complained. I couldn't. Not after watching Big John board the bus after his loss. His face didn't read like a man who had survived a loss. He wore the face of a man who had a survival plan for life. I knew all the great athletes had an inner drive to go over and beyond what would break a normal person, but the perseverance and persistence Big John displayed that day went far beyond what was expected and made him a Mighty Teddy legend.

I had set goals for myself that would one day put me on the same field with young men I'd respected, admired, and even worshipped. I hadn't known that, in wanting to be one of them, to face off against Lions, Tigers, Broncos, Falcons, and so many others, as a Mighty Fighting Teddy,

96

I'd be exposing myself to a level of living that demanded excellence at all times, even during times of adversity. Especially during times of adversity.

Warm-ups were done. It was only a couple minutes from the start of the game. I was now in a cold sweat. Our team captains met Jefferson's team captains at the center of the field. The coin was tossed.

I took my place on the bench, ready to watch the mighty warriors play from the best seat in the house. I was happy to be dressed in the jersey I had dreamed of one day wearing, but I wasn't as ecstatic as expected. Thoughts of John ran through my head. To this day, I still question myself as to whether or not I would have had the same courage to be present myself in the freezing rain, in 10-below zero weather, just after losing the man who had given me life to the great unknown of death.

As much as I don't always want to think about it, everyone is going to live and everyone is going to die. But not everyone gets called up to the starting line. My Grandmother always used to tell us children that we had to take our lumps, then get on with living life. Watching Big John, I was convinced that, at some point in his past, someone must've told him the same. Maybe his dad, the same Mr. Williams who'd stood beside my dad on the day I snuck into practice.

When your number is called, it's up to you to decide to suit up and show up or to sit it out and hope there'll come another chance. It can be tempting to think that when something in our life derails us, if we stop, the whole world is going to stop with us, or wait for us. But that isn't how it happens. There is always someone out there waiting to play in your place.

The rain was pure ice now. The whistle blew to start the game. I watched eleven of our most fearsome players take to the field. Our kicker, Phil Garrison, set the ball on the tee then counted off the number of players on the field. I watched, counting along with him. By my count, I got ten. When I was on the suicide squad, we'd have eleven guys on the field, but I figured that, with these big, imposing, impressive guys, they only needed ten to get the job done.

"McLemore!" I heard a thunderous yell and turned to see Coach Montgomery.

I can't repeat what he said to me that night, due to my limited writing ability and the fact that I don't want to write the kind of words he used for fear people might quote me. But I'm sure you can imagine what a man who used "Shit Fire" as a verb, adjective, and noun might have had to say upon discovering that the game was about to begin and his eleventh man was sitting on the bench, daydreaming.

"Me?" I pointed to my chest.

When I finally realized that I was the missing eleventh man, I ran out onto the field as fast as I could. Lucky for me, the 10-below wind blew the ball off the tee, saving our team from unnecessarily using a time out, and saving my butt from getting kicked off the squad before I'd gotten a chance to play. I'm telling you, if it hadn't been for the north wind blowing that ball off the tee when it did, my story would have ended right there.

Mistakes are an essential part of "The System." It's not whether we mess up, but how we respond to and learn from our inevitable errors, that matters. There is a huge difference between a person who claims ownership of his or her mistakes and one who refuses to admit when he or she is at fault. People who make excuses and blame others for their mental lapses don't learn or evolve.

Wise people have figured out that living life in the driving lane of accountability is the only way to get from where you are to where you want to be. Likewise, in accepting ownership when things don't go the way you want, you can also legitimately accept ownership when things do. Only by acknowledging that you are the source of your experiences, past, present, and future, positive and negative, and that you can choose your actions and attitudes at any time, can you realize your power and potential.

I accepted ownership. My head hadn't been in the game. I'd been so preoccupied with thoughts about what I would do if I was in Big John's place, that I lost sight of my purpose, and almost lost everything I'd worked so hard for.

I'm reminded of the late 90s, when MTV ran a feature story about a young man who was widely credited with taking rap music global. Before this man's impact on the music world, rap had been relegated to "urban America," which was the politically correct way of saying that rap was considered "black music."

Until he came onto the scene, rap artists had been unable to attract white music fans. But this young man, who called himself "M.C. Hammer," had a vision of using his talents to reach people. From the time he was a young boy, Hammer loved music and had a natural aptitude both for vocals and dancing. He danced on the hard streets of Oakland, California, which took him from the floor show of the streets, to being a ball boy for the Oakland A's. At night, he would dance in local nightclubs, where the patrons would stop to watch his electrifying moves. His Johnny-on-the-spot dance skills got him discovered by a talent scout for one of the major recording labels, and, due to the impact he made on the scout, Hammer landed his first deal. He had positioned himself in such a way that the deal he landed was one that would normally have been reserved for groups that had more established names. What that meant was that the record label made a significant investment in him, such that they were incentivized to heavily promote him so they could recoup their investment.

When his first record finally came out, history was made. M.C. Hammer took the music industry – indeed the nation – by storm, with his hit single "You Can't Touch This."

M.C. Hammer was, by most accounts, a good-natured guy. Anyone who had the good fortune to be in his company who needed help or requested a handout would not walk away from Mr. Hammer empty-handed. I know this to be a fact because of my friend Lisa, who, in the mid-1990s, was trying to break into show business. Lisa was by far one of the best female dancers I'd ever seen, and after she was turned down by the producer of the hit show "In Living Color," M.C. Hammer gave her a spot in his dance troupe. Because of his good heart and his eye for talent, Lisa went on to be the featured dancer in the opening to the hit show "Living Single" and later appeared in several music videos, including one with L.L. Cool J. From all reports, M.C. Hammer was a good soul who made it his mission to treat people with love, kindness, and respect. He was able to inspire fifty or more performers to travel around the world with him, and to instill order among a population (creatives) that has a reputation for being notoriously difficult to manage. Hammer set rules that there were to be no drugs in his camp, and that anyone entrusted to him who was underage had a curfew and would be carefully watched and protected from the pain and pitfalls that often follow fortune and fame.

The reason I'm sharing about M.C. Hammer isn't because of what he did, but what he failed to do.

At one time, Hammer was the star of stars. Not only did he make it to the top of the record charts, he stayed there for two years. Hammer was the star of stars. He broke all the current rap-related records, won countless awards, built a $10,000,000 home for himself and his wife, overlooking his old neighborhood, and was ready to go one-on-one with the King of Pop, Michael Jackson, to prove to the world who was the true king of the Big Show. Everyone loved him. Those who were in his world loved him so much that they held tight to his shirttails as his shooting star soared high above the clouds. Then, those same beloved friends and fans who rode Hammer's coattails to stardom let go and watched as his star fell hopelessly back to earth. Once the money well dried up, those he had helped turned a blind eye to his need.

While watching the MTV broadcast, I was so touched by this once iconic, now disgraced man's personal story, that I was in the process of writing a check to help him and his family (At that time, I didn't have much, but his story moved me), when, before I could finish filling out my check, Hammer told his interviewer he didn't want anyone to feel sorry for him. He said that everything that had happened to him had happened because he let it. No one was to blame but himself. His downfalls and shortcomings were a result of his failings, and any successes that were to come would be a result of his ability to bounce back.

I never wrote the check, but I also never forgot the powerful way in which M.C. Hammer held himself accountable. I don't think his story is any different than the story of any other man or woman who made their dream a reality, or who, upon the realization of his or her heart's desires, lost everything. The uniqueness of M. C. Hammer's story was that he took full responsibility for his fall from stardom. There were a lot of people he could've blamed, but he never stooped to that. As an outsider, however, I was all too willing to be indignant on the rapper's behalf.

I've observed a tendency among Black Americans to hold our people accountable to much higher standards than those of any other culture. In most cases, as a race, probably due to the system of slavery, we have been so separated from each other and ourselves that instead of lifting one another up, we're all too ready to tear each other down. We tend to form opinions, which we then relay – loudly and often – to anyone who will listen about what people like M.C. Hammer must give back to the community, or what they should or shouldn't do with their money. Even though he exhibited admirable character throughout his career, those same people who made him the super star that he was were all too quick to fault him.

Hammer's story was a textbook example of what happens when your own people don't think you've given enough. I believe from his interview, and from what I learned from people who knew him personally, that because his music crossed over to white America at a time when black fans and other rappers thought that rap was only for blacks, by and large, the African American community labeled him a sellout. Other black rappers put him down, calling him a "paper rapper."

Sure, Hammer made mistakes. He mismanaged his money and was a poor judge of character, but he was an honorable man and didn't deserve to be taken down. When a big shot like Hammer, who came from the school of hard knocks, is willing to open a couple of doors for the guy who is coming up behind him, and struggling to make it in this cool and calculating world, he deserves to hold onto his dreams.

Unfortunately, "The System" doesn't discriminate. When we fail to use discernment, or abdicate responsibility to people who can't be trusted, losing everything becomes a very real possibility.

For those who think money is a "cure-all," here is something my two caregivers, my grandmother and my grandfather, once said to me. "I could give you money, but that will never help solve a problem. It will only help you to avoid the problem for the moment."

A dollar bill has no loyalty. Mr. Hammer learned that the hard way. He also learned that "friends" who flock to your success aren't necessarily going to be there during moments of failure. That said, there are many, many people in this world who can be trusted. I learned the importance of teamwork on the football field, but over the course of my sixty years, I've been blessed to find myself surrounded by people in whom I could trust, and who could likewise trust in me, but that meant giving up running with those who would put themselves in situations where they'd be forced to run from the Chains of Rap Brown and surrounding myself with people whose values aligned with mine. There was Jason, of course. True friends and teammates, he and I were invested in lifting each other up. On the day of my first game, Jason was in the game as well, both of us side by side. Only, this time we weren't running away from anyone. We were running toward the end zone.

My father, who had never seen me play, sat proudly in the cold, wet stands. My older brother Leroy Jr (who couldn't afford the price of the ticket), stood bravely on the hill, overlooking the field on the northwest corner of the Welcome Stadium wall.

Looking back, I have trouble remembering the exact sequence of events that day. I was so present to each play, so engaged in the moment, so intent on proving myself, that the game became a blur. There was one moment, however, that I can't forget. It was the moment I was running downfield when an oblong ball seemed to descend, like magic, from the sky.

Those tip drills paid off. I reached my arms out, caught the ball in my underclassman hands, tucked it beneath one arm, and took off with all the speed I could muster. No one could catch me. I'd practiced in the cold, the mud, and the heat. I'd sacrificed myself on the suicide squad. I'd internalized the fundamentals. I ran even faster than the night I'd run for my life, Jason just behind me, with the Chains of Rap Brown hot on our heels. By comparison, the sprint to the end zone felt effortless. The touchdown, and the extra point the kicker, Phil Garrison, scored put our team in the lead and earned me a starting spot from then on.

I'd officially become one of the guys I'd longed to be.

CHAPTER 27

THE KEYS TO THE SYSTEM

On nearly every job application, there's a space that asks you to fill in your experience. Prospective employers want to know not only that you have acquired the information necessary to obtain the requisite qualifications for a position, but that you can apply what you've learned in real life situations. Of course, there may be some exceptions to this rule.

There's a company in New York City that sent out a memo that stated that they would only be hiring from Ivy League schools. That means graduates of over 300 other accredited schools in this country (very qualified young men and women) will be sending their resumes to this company (which I will leave nameless), only to have their résumés get put in file 13, the waste paper basket. They say that employers are supposed to be equal opportunity employers, careful not to discriminate against anyone based on race, creed or color, but there are loopholes in every system. There are actually people out there with degrees, who try to see how to get around and over on this System and still be called equal opportunity employers. There are organizations that won't even consider hiring anyone who may not fit in with the mighty all-boys club that many would claim doesn't exist, but which clearly does, no matter what you're told.

The reason this matter is that, when I write about navigating "The System" from within, I want to be clear that I'm not naïve. There may be avenues of exploration that are unavailable to you because of factors outside of your control – age, race, gender, upbringing, geographical, socioeconomic status... The list is long.

I know all too well about discrimination. I grew up a poor, motherless black kid in Dayton, Ohio. However, even if life's deck is stacked against you, that by no means gives you a permission slip to give up striving. If anything, when all you have going for you is intellect and ingenuity, whenever opportunities arise – which they will, if you work for them – you must capitalize on them.

I wasn't born with a silver spoon. If I had a spoon at all, I had a plastic one. Plus, with all the siblings I had, I'm sure I was expected to share it. Yet, I've been able to achieve great things.

Some of my success was made possible through physical rigor, most through diligent practice. I was far from a natural superstar. I wasn't especially tall or well-muscled. I had speed, and I worked hard. I worked hard in school, too. (Despite having ADHD, with which I was diagnosed just before my 50th birthday). Yet, none of my achievements will ever surpass the moment when I personally brought my youngest son into the world.

To be competitive, education is essential. There may be those who drop out of school and still manage to make it big, but I learned from my grandfather that knowledge is the critical key to unlocking doors. Most, if not all, successful people, whether they boast a standard educational pedigree, are avid seekers of information.

Talent and skill are two of the greatest misunderstood concepts for people who are trying to excel. Talent can only get a person so far in life. Even the most naturally talented among us need to acquire the capacity to capitalize on that talent. A good education will allow a dreamer's talent to take flight naturally. Skill is only developed by hours, and years, of mastering your craft.

My Uncle Bill would say "You need to put yourself in a position where your talent can be found, because most smart people, surround themselves with likeminded people." I've found that like-mindedness is critical. If you want to make it to the pinnacle of achievement, surround yourself not only with quality people, but with genuine people, which are those who have your best interests in mind.

I used to question myself because whatever wisdom I'd acquired had come from the wisdom I'd gained in life. I'd graduated Central State University, sure, yet somehow, I felt as if the "really smart" among us were the Ivy League graduates with strings of initials after their names. That wasn't me. Even so, I can't even begin to tell you how many opportunities my college education has made available to me. I've gone places and met people I wouldn't have ever met if I'd stopped at a high school diploma or dropped out like some of the young people I've known (some of whom are members of my own family).

It's true that in my generation there were a lot of big-named people who, when you heard them tell their stories, didn't have much by way of an education. But nowadays it seems you need a master's degree just to get your foot in the corporate door, to apply for an entry level job. Besides, I'd put good money down on a bet that, if you were to go down the list of Who's Who and identify anyone who's "made it" without the proper educational pedigree, you'd find that every last one of them employs highly creative, highly intelligent, highly educated people and that it's these people who help them run their businesses and expand their brands. At the same time, many of those who received stellar educational opportunities, dropped out of some of the best school in this country to build brands like Facebook and Amazon. The path need not always be linear, but the acquisition of information and the synergy between analysis and application are essential.

Receive as much education as you can while at the same time expanding your vision far beyond the hallways of the educational system.

Education is an invaluable part of life's system. It may not be everything, yet it gives you the opportunity to obtain the fundamentals that will help you succeed throughout your life. Consider learning the equivalent of practice. School may not be the big game, the one where winner takes all, but it's necessary if you hope to make it off the bench and onto the field.

Most successful people don't hang around people who will bring them down, people that will pull them down. I can attest to that. There are not many of my friends who don't have a degree hanging somewhere in their homes, or offices, or buried in some back-room closet. This isn't a result of snobbery or elitism. Considering where I come from, and what I've been up against over the course of my life, and the mistakes I've made along the way, I have no room to think I'm better or worse than anyone else. I am, however, interested in being around people who will challenge and uplift me.

The people in your sphere of influence – those who are influenced by and who influence you – are critically important. I know this from personal experience, and I've witnessed it in others, sometimes with devastating consequences.

At the time I began to outline my notes for this book, my seventeen-year-old daughter came to me to tell me she'd arrived at a crossroad in her life. While living with her mother in Dayton, she had been associating with a group of people who devalued themselves and each other. As a result, she'd become one of our country's many statistics.

Despite the opportunities that awaited her, my daughter had gotten pregnant. While still in high school, with less than a year to go, when she was nothing but a babe herself, she was going to be a mother.

I thought about omitting this part of my story, because I have a great relationship with my daughter and didn't want to damage it by sharing about her early life experiences, but I realized that hers is a powerful example. What my daughter went through speaks to the power of choice and is a perfect illustration of how life is full of opportunities for growth.

The decisions my daughter made placed a burden on her and her unborn child. I flashed back to the week I visited her at school and the toddlers tagging along with their teenaged mothers. I couldn't do anything to save her, yet I flew to Ohio to have a face-to-face with my daughter and the expectant father, who at that time was only sixteen himself. I took both of them to a bookstore, bought them a couple of books about parenting for them to read so they would understand what they were getting themselves into, and so they could have access to information that was coming from experts, rather than a highly emotional father.

After the bookstore, I took them to one of Dayton's most upscale restaurants. They both placed their orders with their eyes averted, as if they couldn't wait till, I was back on a plane to

New York, sparing them having to listen to whatever they thought I might say. But my intention wasn't to tell them that what they had done was either right or wrong. I wanted to prepare them for what they would face if they allowed my daughter's pregnancy to derail their educations. To my surprise, when I asked what their plans were as far as school was concerned, they both responded that they were going to finish school, which I thought doubtful considering neither had gone to school even when they weren't expecting to be parents.

My week-long student shadowing had been temporarily effective, but without ongoing parental supervision, my daughter had reverted to old habits.

I sat and listened, and held back on the advice I had prepared on the plane trip down, as the sixteen-year-old young man who'd impregnated my daughter told me that, after he finished high school, he planned to go off to college. I looked from him to my daughter, who didn't appear to be reacting to this news. I waited for his words to register with her. She took a bite. He continued talking about his collegiate aspirations.

No longer able to keep my mouth shut, I said, "I hope you heard what the father of your baby just said."

"I heard what he said," my daughter responded.

But she didn't hear what I heard. To me, it felt as if her boyfriend was stating that she was on her own. He wanted a better life for himself. The fact that she was having his child wasn't going to hold him back. I asked her to think long and hard about what they were about to do, creating a life before they had a chance to create a life for themselves.

I held on to my thoughts, because the times I have spoken to my young athletes about being accountable and responsible. To my knowledge, it is not the norm for a someone who graduated college to marry a high school dropout, let alone stay around long enough to be a full-time parent and a positive example to a child.

Harsh, but true, "those who go out and make more of themselves, don't hang around long with the people who accept less."

As my grandmother so eloquently put it, "You know better, you do better, and one day people will pay to stand in line to hear what you know." "Just do better, baby."

But my conversation with them was for naught. Everything I said fell on deaf ears. It didn't even phase the young man when I handed him the restaurant bill. He simply looked at me with bright eyes and of course, I fell for it, paying the entire amount myself.

As predicted, my daughter and her child's father broke up. She dropped out of school sometime after and as for him, I am not sure.

I wished I could've coached her into greatness, the way Coach Russo and Coach Montgomery coached me. Maybe, I was too close to the situation, or maybe too far, but I couldn't get through to her and, as a result, her life as a child was a lot harder than it had to be, but she's my daughter, she's tough, I just ask God to watch over my baby girl.

If the truth were to be told, I wasn't as academically oriented in high school as I am today. I got decent grades, and, after I got into college, I regularly made the Dean's List. But I wasn't the type of kid who sailed through my studies. I can attribute some of that to ADHD, an initial learning curve, and grief. My first quarter of my freshman year of college, my Uncle Bill was killed. Losing him was a devastating blow to me and to the entire family, especially considering how it happened. Uncle Bill, my mentor and best friend, was shot to death on New Year's morning by his cheating wife's dope-dealing boyfriend, which led me into a two-year state of depression. Yet, I didn't let the pain or loss derail me from my studies. Doing well in school was a matter of personal pride. Even so, as an adult, I'm a much better student now.

I study life as diligently as I once studied football. I read at least two books a week, not to mention endless articles, both in print and online. For the most part, I like to think I can hold my own with guys from Ivy League schools. Many of my friends have degrees from Harvard, Yale, and the rest, and we regularly enlighten one another about a multitude of subjects. When there's a situation where I find myself at a loss, I pull out a pad and paper and take notes, then I do research on whatever has me stumped. I ask questions and am relentless in my pursuit of answers.

I believe today's students have to take life on much sooner and more seriously than I did. Without a good secondary and post-graduate education, it will be nearly impossible to meet the challenges of our ever-changing world. Yet, a person's path doesn't need to be perfect or linear. Despite how much I thought I knew when I sat across the table from my daughter and her impending baby daddy, she has exceeded my most fervent hopes for her. In 2010, I watched her walk across the stage to get her college degree, while her three children sat watching, as in awe of their mother as I was of my daughter. Yes, she dropped out of school, but she went back and got her GED and has since gone on to build an incredible life for herself.

My daughter has proven smarter than her old man. Her grit has changed the way I look at the potential of a human being. Now, when it comes to my kids, I hold my hand over my mouth and take notes. It's well worth the trade-off. Because of my daughter's decisions, decisions I was sure would hold her back from accomplishing her dreams, I now have three wonderful grandchildren whom I love to death and whose achievements never cease to amaze me.

CHAPTER 28

IN THE REAL WORLD, THE SYSTEM IS ALL ABOUT LIFE

Most of us know the difference between what is right and what is wrong. We've learned enough of the rules to understand that in life, as in football, we can't be offsides without earning ourselves a penalty flag and putting ourselves and our teams in jeopardy.

The more clarity you have on who you want to be and what matters to you, and the more you commit yourself to navigating within "The System" to authentically show up as the winner you are capable of being, the more unable you will be of acting out of alignment with your values and goals. The values I do my best to live by are honesty, integrity, reliability and faith. Any time I think about straying from these, I experience an immediate recoiling in my gut.

I had no idea the day I stood in front of Coach Montgomery as the dust succumbed to his will and his voice boomed out with resonance, clearly stating what was expected of a Mighty Teddy that I was forever committing to a life of greatness. All I knew was that I wanted to be the kind of guy who could walk the halls of Roosevelt High with his head high, his shoulders back, and his jersey telegraphing his success.

I hope that you will look in the mirror and ask yourself some of life's most meaningful questions: *Am I living the life I want to live? Where am I going? Will I be happy there, and can I make a difference? Is what I'm doing adding value to the planet? If not, am I ready to change my behavior, and if I do, where will this change take me? Am I prepared for greatness?*

Think about whether the life you're currently living is reflective of your capabilities. Usually, it won't be. Most of us suffer from a tendency to play small, to settle for the freshman squad when, with some diligent effort, we could make it to varsity. Worse yet, some of us never try out at all, or tell ourselves we're content to sit on the sidelines – or even in the stands.

Life is not a spectator sport. If you pay attention to the feeling in your gut, you'll come to realize that it's calling you to strive for what you want, even if you're not yet sure what that is. Instincts and common sense are your best indicators of where it is you do and don't want to go.

Study what they're telling you. I don't mean the momentary impulses toward short-term pleasure, but the deep feelings that magnetize us toward what is in our highest good and repel us from what will only hurt us in the end.

One morning in 1995 or 1996, as I was training my friend and client, Mr. John Emmerling, (an author and advertising executive), he began to tell me about a lecture he had attended the previous weekend. The keynote speaker was Mr. Jack Rudd, the son of real estate billionaire, Samuel Rudd. When asked the secret of his success, Jack's response was "Read a book, take a walk, make a friend."

I wrote his wise words in my journal. Since then, I've internalized them. I encourage you to do the same. Read the words, read them again, recite them with your eyes closed. Ponder their meaning and internalize it. If you're somewhere where you can meditate on Rudd's words, repeating them over and over like a mantra, let them flow through you until you have a visceral response.

I won't tell you how his words resonated within me. I want you to have your own experience of letting this simple, common sense strategy impact you. But, whatever your experience, do let it impact you.

If you do the math, employing a simple strategy for living creates a winning equation. Simply by having a clear plan of action, and executing on that plan, you can both get what you want and help others in the process. Just as bad habits can become ingrained, so can good ones. Develop winning routines and you will become a winner.

I like to say, "Fail till you win." Whether in the arena of life or the arena in football, you'll get hit again and again. All you have to do is move the ball farther downfield, score whenever possible, and keep your adversaries from getting the upper hand.

Before I became a member of the Mighty Teddies football team, I didn't give any thought to the consequences of my actions, or how they would affect the people I claimed to love. The fact that I lied my way onto the team was proof in and of itself that I wasn't living in integrity. Luckily, Coach Russo's willingness to take a chance on a lowly freshman forever altered the trajectory of my life. Instead of calling me on my lie, he saved me.

Pops used to tell us, "If you obey the law, you never have to worry about being in trouble." (Unless you're a black man walking the streets of New York, or driving in the town of Phoenixville, PA. But that's another story for another time).

I think that one of the most prevalent mistakes people make is that they confuse intelligence with good judgment. The therapist at Bryn Mawr rehab that was treating me for my March 2nd, 2019 concussion reminded me everyday "Don't let your personality override your intelligence." There are a lot of people out there who have high intelligence and are notoriously poor in judgment. Conversely, there are many (and I would consider myself to be in this category) who leverage reasonable amounts of intellect to generate above average success.

There are a lot of books out there that will tell you they have the 6-, 7-, 8-, 9-, or 10-step program to success, and if you do the steps that are outlined in that book, you can be just as successful as the person who wrote the book. These books sell you on the idea that, simply by understanding whatever they're attempting to convey, you can live happily ever after. I'm not buying. There's a difference between information and internalization. Let's say you read that book that promises to change your life. Nine times out of ten, a few weeks later, the book will be all but forgotten and your personal habits will have kicked back in. Pretty soon, you'll be looking for yet another book in the hopes that it will be THE book that will take you from where you are to where you want to be. Let me offer a different alternative. Turn to my words, written by a guy who is just like you, not famous, not born with any particular advantages, but who has applied certain systems to his life and can show you how to move out of the realm of mere education and into the lived space of experience. Take a risk. Create a strategy to bring you from where you are now to where you want to go.

Ask yourself *What do I want most out of life?*

Write down your answer. Then, write down a plan of action that will take you from where you are now to where you want to be. If you're not certain how to get there, maybe you need to do some research, employ a coach, or form a group of trusted friends that can act as a team by challenging you to play harder than if you were in the game alone.

It's not about the money you can make, or the big house you can have, or the trip you've always dreamed of taking. It's about your willingness to create the life you want. By remaining motivated and going through life with blinders on, focused on what's straight ahead, you'll get what you want. Stay true to the course.

I owe the game of football everything. The road I was on before I became a Mighty Teddy would've led to addiction, incarceration, or death. I was blessed. God put me in a place where there was love, structure, and direction. He also gave me the gift of speed. Then again, I believe God gives every one of us gifts. If we capitalize on them, we will achieve everything we want – and more. We owe it to ourselves and others to utilize our innate talents and abilities to do great things, not only for us, but for our fellow men and women.

Edward Howe, the writer, wrote, "Life is like a game of cards. Reliability is the Ace. Industry the king, Politeness the queen, and Thrift is the Jack." To make the most out of life, we need to play the cards we draw to advantage. And every day, as the game proceeds, we will find ourselves discovering that we hold Aces, Kings, Queens or Jacks. It's up to us when and how to play them.

Make "The System" work for, and not against, you. Make the most of what you have. Stop reminding yourself of what you don't. We all get the same 24 hours each day, and, as far as I'm aware, we only get one chance at life. Each day is an opportunity to score another touchdown.

CHAPTER 29

NOTHING TO FEAR, BUT FEAR ITSELF

In May 2019, as I sat staring at my blank computer screen, my head throbbing, I could barely form a coherent thought, let alone write something that'd be worth reading. For months, I'd been living with the never-ending pain of a concussion, which I got during an accident at work. I refused to give up. Writing this book had become my dream and I'd never been one to relinquish a dream, or to let up on the attainment of it.

> *What happens to a dream deferred?*
> *Does it dry up*
> *Like a raisin in the sun?*
> *Or fester like a sore—*
> *And then run?*
> *Does it stink like rotten meat?*
> *Or crust and sugar over—*
> *like a syrupy sweet?*
> *Maybe it just sags*
> *like a heavy load.*
> *Or does it explode?*
> *Langston Hughes*

My older son, Alexander, sat on the couch waiting for me to take a break. Ever since he was three and I had that moment of prioritizing writing over him, I'd vowed that the time I spent working on this book wouldn't interfere with the time I spent with my children. I once said to a friend that a moment not spent with your child is a moment forever lost in time. My son was now twenty-five, far from a child, and I was on the verge of a new thought. Whatever it was would have to wait.

I turned away from the computer, wrapped my arms around his solid, 6 foot-one frame and told him my writing could wait. I needed a break anyway. The head-pounding was relentless and so was the nagging guilt. I'd started to second-guess myself, not about what I'd written, but about how my dad would feel about some of the things I'd said. He was still alive at the time and his feelings mattered to me.

I love my dad. When I look back at what he tried to do for me, versus what I thought he should have done, I understand that he did what he thought was right. Even though he never said it, he had a hard life. Now that I'm a father, I see that he did the best he could. I can't fault any man for choices he made without having the foresight, knowledge, and experience to envision their consequences.

My dad did what he knew how to do. If he'd known better, he'd have done better. He wasn't perfect, but neither was he a deadbeat dad. I'm glad he stayed with us kids and never left town.

Looking at my own kids – Lakisha, Alex, Theo and Jillian – I know that my children's judgments of me will forever mean more to me than anyone else's. The four of them keep me in a constant state of self-check. I find that, as a parent, I'm forever looking over my shoulder, trying to see how all the things I do or don't do affect them. I'm constantly assessing my actions and inactions and the impact they make on the ones I love most.

I don't believe my dad ever looked back to do a self-check. I don't mean that as a form of recrimination. The things that matter to parents today didn't matter then. There wasn't the same level of awareness, or sensitivity. I'm not so sure that was a bad thing. Having Leroy McLemore Sr. for a father made me the man I am today. His lack of action propelled me to be always moving, always striving. Without the examples of Pops, Uncle Bill, Ron, and Dad, showing me what I wanted to emulate and what I wanted to avoid, I couldn't have evolved into a person I am proud of. Sure, I'll always have room to grow, but my examples of masculinity have shaped me in too many ways to enumerate.

Although I couldn't have identified it at the time, I'm fairly certain my father was afraid. We're all afraid. Fear is a necessary part of life. But football taught me to relate to fear differently, by preparing for every eventuality.

In the early 1990s, I took my own personal poll of a hundred highly successful people, and I asked them what they feared most. My reason for polling well-to-do people, rather than struggling people, was that I had no interest in learning how to be poor and depressed and stay that way. I wanted to understand and replicate the steps required to achieve greatness. So, I found one hundred successful and emotionally rich people in New York City, and when I evaluated my findings, what I discovered was that the things they feared the most were the loss of love, poor health, the loss of a child, the loss of a job, or losing their social identity. Those fears make sense to me. The fears that don't make sense are the worries that arise with the inevitable, every day, play-by-play of life. It's all too easy to get lost in anxiety, then fail to take action. I've learned not to stress about that which I can't control.

In July 1997, there was a huge UPS strike. I had just gotten my first publishing deal by a major publishing house, St. Martin's Press of New York. *Letters to Elvis* was due to be released three weeks before the anniversary of the 20th year of Elvis' death. The book was the first of its kind. No one had ever written a book based on the admiration of a star's fans before, and I was excited to see how it'd be received. I had interviewed or read letters from over five thousand people who had been personally touched by the man and his music. But the strike halted the delivery of the book to the stores that had ordered it. It didn't matter that I had a major write-up in *Life Magazine*, where over 20 million people had read in advance about my book coming out, or that I had been interviewed on national radio shows and TV. It didn't matter that I got calls from family and friends, both in the US and abroad, requesting copies of the book. My dream lay stored somewhere in a warehouse in South Carolina. August 16th (Elvis's anniversary) came and went. Like any other event in my life, I always look for the light in the darkest part of the rooms. This was a wake-up call to what I believe young people will have to face in the very near future. Forget what you've heard or been taught and the present job market. The job market is changing even as you read the words on this page. The results or the resolution of the UPS strike are irrelevant. Yes, the postal workers eventually resumed their duties, but by then my book had become old news. My message had lost its momentum.

I predict that the future corporate system will function on a "no full-time job or career track employee" system. Rather, it will operate on a job-to-job system, where work will be farmed out to avoid paying the big bucks for overtime and insurance. The days of retiring with a gold watch and monthly check are over.

Years ago, I had a conversation with my good friend Matthew in which he told me that he believed that by the year 2010, 75% of the top jobs in our country would be permanent part-time work; that competition for work will be so intense that people would need to enter into a lottery-type system to obtain jobs, or worse, bidding wars could develop among people looking for work. Clearly, his predictions have not come to pass, but that's the thing about predictions. There's no telling what will happen, but that doesn't mean we can't position ourselves for any eventuality.

At some time in my past, I was a futurist. I had to be. This book wouldn't exist if I hadn't had the foresight to write down and record the important events in my life. Sometimes, life's unpredictabilities tackle you when you least suspect it.

Letters to Elvis never had the impact it could have, but that didn't stop me from fulfilling my dreams of publication. When my next book idea came about, I didn't even entertain the idea of not committing those thoughts down to paper. I continued onward with that dream (*Sprinkles*) and then, subsequently, with this one.

The athletes I know, myself included, look at fear as an adventure, a wondrous journey, filled with exciting moments. Being afraid becomes like sitting in the first seat of a super roller coaster, throwing both hands up and enjoying the ride. But everyday people don't think like athletes. At least, not often. Then, there are the times when athletes are the times when athletes are tempted to succumb to the lure of mediocrity.

When I had my first son, I wondered what would happen if I failed. Would someone show up out of nowhere and take my kid away until I became a good parent? No. And there would be no do-overs. A baby comes into this world totally perfect. It has all these little toes, two little legs, arms and fingers, perfect in every way. If you've never seen a child come into the world, you should. The experience is astonishing. From the very first breath that baby takes, he or she is fighting to live. And, although I have no way of knowing whether or not an infant feels fear, it seems clear that every infant wants to ride life's roller coaster in the front seat with both hands up, screaming its head off, because it's on a journey filled with excitement and adventure. At birth, a child only sees in black and white, until he or she starts to see in color. They don't require an abundance of stimulation. All they want is to be loved and taken care of. They are as perfect as perfect can get, with none of life's many hang-ups. They're a blank slate, ready to be taught the strategies and systems that will assure their happiness and success or victims of their parents' unpreparedness who aren't given the tools to make it and as such are destined to fail, unless they study hard and learn the game themselves.

CHAPTER 30

ANYTHING'S POSSIBLE

My personality today is a direct reflection of the way I learned to play the game. Consistency, durability, dependability, self-control and mental concentration were all things I was taught first in practice, then during play. As a young man, I was angry and didn't know it. The feelings of being abandoned by my mother and dropped off on the doorsteps of my grandparents left me wanting to reach out and hit something. Football helped me find an outlet for my rage. Unbeknownst to me at the time, the game demanded I evolve beyond my circumstances.

In my heart, I always knew I wanted to be more than I was. But I didn't understand my situation then, the way I do today. Because I had such a great view of the downside of my life and the hell, I thought I was living in, the view of the upside began to come in more clearly each day.

When you open your eyes and face what you think you're angry about, you may come to find out (as I did), that it's not really anger at all. It's hurt. Under the careful care of the coaches and my teammates, I soon began to get the validation and positive sense of self that I had been missing. When you're abandoned by your mother when you're only eight years old, it's easy to give up on yourself. In football, giving up isn't an option. We wore our attitudes like permanent jerseys. The identity of a Mighty Teddy became one that could never be taken off. So many players impacted the way I think and live. Larry Hightower motivated by example, Big John suited up and showed up, no matter what the circumstances, and Kelli Spicer was a true team player who gave 110% all the time, which made up for his lack of size and speed.

Anyone who succeeds against all odds is what I refer to as a "possibility thinker." They believe that, if you want more, you must come to practice early and stay late. They know that what you put into life is what you get out of it, and they practice harder than anyone else, smiling through it, and contributing when and what they can, no matter what.

After football season ended, I went out for track. I'd always been a fast runner and, after experiencing the rush of athleticism and comradery of being on a team I knew I'd be a lifelong competitive athlete. My track coach, the late Don Mitchell, used to tell us, "When you're out in front, never look back over your shoulder." He said to stay focused on what was ahead and that, if we took our eyes off where we were going, our competition would pass us by. This straight-ahead thinking has enabled me to remain fixed on the prize.

Unfortunately, during the long, lonely hours, days, weeks, months, and years I worked on this book, I had no other option but to look over my shoulder, examining what was and remembering the pain of my mother packing up and leaving town. Until I found belonging in football, her abandonment was a wound that made me feel unloved and alone. Confronting the reality of my childhood in the inked words on the page, I realized that I was one pen stroke short of being a child of the welfare system, the social picture of the ills of crime, another motherless child – in short, another statistic.

I've come to believe that all people carry around some degree of burden. We build internal walls to justify the hate, anger and resentment we carry toward ourselves and others. We give more power to painful situations than circumstances warrant and end up dragging our pasts behind us like dead weight. Is it any wonder that self-destructive behavior is so prevalent? The past is the past. It can't hurt us anymore unless we can't let it go, in which case our previous experiences aren't what's hurting us. We're hurting ourselves. Our perpetual remembering creates self-inflicted pain. What's more, by always looking back, we rob ourselves of seeing clearly what's ahead.

Yet, feelings demand to be felt. We can't run around them. We must take the hard hits, get up, dust ourselves off, then get back in the game.

When I tried to detach my heart from the woman who gave me life, I told myself the old cliché: "Out of sight, out of mind." That held true until 1985 when my mother rose from the dead and relocated back to Dayton, Ohio. At the time of her return, I had been recovering from a head injury I'd sustained while at spring training. I'd been working as the personal trainer for superstar shortstop Julio Franco, of the Cleveland Indians (as well as many of his teammates) when a 150-pound weight stack fell on my head and knocked me out. The injury had temporarily erased much of my memory, but it hadn't erased the picture of the woman who stood on the porch of my grandmother's neighbor, calling my name.

The day I saw Norma Jean standing outside, the hurt I thought I'd gotten over returned. Actually, I'm pretty sure it had never left. I was a grown man with a family of my own and here was my mother attempting to pick up where she had left off. My brothers and sisters had no problem with her unannounced return, but I wished she'd never come back. I'd written her out of my life story. Or had I? My mother's reappearance sparked a whole new level of second-guessing what I was feeling. All the negative energy that had lain dormant in my soul resurfaced. I had to face what I'd run from.

It wasn't until I started to outline this book that I discovered I still harbored animosity – a lot of animosity – toward my mother. Football taught me that the best way to deal with pain was to face it. I began to share the contents of this book with my mother. In one of our very polite, yet tension-filled conversations, she told me something that forever changed my relationship with her, and my relationship with my past.

"You know, Kevin," she said, "no matter how nicely we speak to each other, whenever we talk, there comes a point in the conversation when you somehow manage to hit me with a sucker punch."

She told me that she always knew it would be coming at some point or another, but for reasons unknown, she couldn't seem to get out of its way. So, she took each hit on the chin.

After we ended that conversation, I sat in a dark room alone with my thoughts and did a lot of soul-searching. I knew that whatever barbed comments I'd made were evidence that I was still giving the past power. I had never really let go. I don't know if I wanted my mother to say she was sorry for leaving us kids and ask for my forgiveness, or if I wanted to rub in her face all that I'd become, while letting her know that she'd played no part in my success. I thought that by being hard-hearted, I was taking power away from her when, in fact, I was only giving her more.

My unwillingness to let go of blame and my insistence on holding on to the pain created an emotional junkyard within me. Debris piled up. I'd convinced myself I was the bigger person. I could not have been more wrong. I took a look in the metaphorical mirror and knew that it was time for me to pay attention to my own message and eat crow. To say what I mean and mean what I say. To stop throwing sucker punches. That was the day I finally let go. I forgave my mother and I resolved that, moving forward, I would practice kindness and love.

The next time my mother and I spoke, I promised her I would never hit her with another sucker punch. "But, in case I accidentally forget," I said, "if you see it coming, please duck, because I will always have to live with the fact that those events in my life did happen, but it's up to me to choose how I feel and react today."

I used to ask myself what my life would have been like if my mother had stayed. But looking at the life I've lived and the life I have today, and knowing the crossroads I've faced and the adversities I've overcome, I believe that her leaving was the best thing she could have ever done. Her absence forced me to be a stronger man and gave me the desire to fight for a better life. Even though I still longed for a mother's love, I can say without reservation that I came to love her fully and completely. Not for being an exemplary parent, but for giving me life. I'm a good man. I've always been a good man. And I'm grateful to my parents for everything they did and didn't give me.

Back in the days when I was playing football, I used to watch the cameras as they panned down the bench over on the sidelines. I always envied those guys who would wave and shout out "Hi, Mom!"

That was never me. I did have people in the stands, though. I had Grandma, Pops, Uncle Bill, Ron and sometimes my dad. And I had my teammates. I was loved. Today, I see my mother and my cup runs over with love. I know that, although she may not have been there in the stands when I was on the field, the next time greatness comes my way, she will be in the stands when I was on the field, the next time greatness comes my way, she will be in the audience and I'll look over at her, my adoring, if long-absent, spectator, wave, and say, "Hi, Mom."

CHAPTER 31

WHAT I BELIEVE: MY CREDO

A lot of wonderful people have impacted my life. The lessons they've taught me have shaped not only how I think, but how I live. It's not so much what they told me that made a difference, just as it won't be what I'm telling you that leads to improvements in your life. It's implementing a set of core values and disciplining myself to live them out that has led me to realize my dreams, one after another. Live not to be ordinary, but to live an extraordinary life.

Pops once said that if everyone would pick three of the Ten Commandments to live by and follow them with 100% commitment, the world would be a better place. I've always felt as if there was something magical about the number seven. There are seven colors in a rainbow, seven musical notes, seven wonders of the world, seven digits in a phone number (not including area code) …

I've compiled a list of as many meaningful credos as I can think of and even included some blank space at the end for you to write in any you might not see that speak to you. My invitation would be to identify seven of these statements that you want to live by, check them off, then write them down in a journal and spend every day from this one until your last living out those beliefs.

- Happiness is a decision. I will decide to be happy.
- Motivation starts the moment I open my eyes.
- What I perceive is my reality. If I don't like my reality, I will alter my perception.
- When you know better, you do better. I will acquire knowledge daily.
- True power comes from compassion and forgiveness.
- A positive attitude is essential.
- Excuses only sound good to the person making them. I resolve to let go of excuses.
- I will respect every human life.
- If a door doesn't open, it's not the door's fault. There is something blocking it from opening. I will identify that block and remove it.

- Facebook, Instagram, and Twitter are distractions. I will not allow social media to distract me from actively participating in life.
- Difficult roads often lead to beautiful destinations.
- Excellence takes dedication, desire, self-discipline, sacrifice and determination.
- The only thing that is universally equal is time. Everybody gets the same 24 hours.
- Friendship is important. No matter what is happening in my life, I will make time for friends.
- Failure is not permanent. It is only temporary. I resolve to fall forward, get up, and keep going.
- I will put my heart and soul into everything I do.
- Fear is not real, it's a by-product of the limits of my imagination. I will not let fear consume me and will choose to live fearlessly.
- My life becomes better by making other people's lives better. Reach one teach one.
- Being realistic is the surest way to mediocrity. I will dare to be unreasonable.
- Dreams without goals are just dreams. They will never come to life. I resolve to attach goals, a well-developed system in place to reach of my dreams.
- I will take responsibility for my life. Be accountable.
- Procrastination is the first door that opens to mediocrity, take your hand off the snooze button.
- I will put God first and allow His directives to guide me.

- _____

- _____

- _____

- _____

- _____

- _____

- _____

- _____

- _____

Made in the USA
Middletown, DE
21 January 2021